Kaplan Publishing are constantly finding new ways to support students looking for exam success and our online resources really do add an extra dimension to your studies.

This book comes with free MyKaplan online resources so that you can study anytime, anywhere. **This free online resource is not sold separately and is included in the price of the book.**

Having purchased this book, you have access to the following online study materials:

CONTENT	AAT	
	Text	Kit
Electronic version of the book	✓	✓
Knowledge Check tests with instant answers		✓
Mock assessments online	✓	✓
Material updates	✓	✓

How to access your online resources

Received this book as part of your Kaplan course?
If you have a MyKaplan account, your full online resources will be added automatically, in line with the information in your course confirmation email. If you've not used MyKaplan before, you'll be sent an activation email once your resources are ready.

Bought your book from Kaplan?
We'll automatically add your online resources to your MyKaplan account. If you've not used MyKaplan before, you'll be sent an activation email.

Bought your book from elsewhere?
Go to **www.mykaplan.co.uk/add-online-resources**
Enter the ISBN number found on the title page and back cover of this book.
Add the unique pass key number contained in the scratch panel below.
You may be required to enter additional information during this process to set up or confirm your account details.

This code can only be used once for the registration of this book online. This registration and your online content will expire when the examinations covered by this book have taken place. Please allow one hour from the time you submit your book details for us to process your request.

Please scratch the film to access your unique code.

Please be aware that this code is case-sensitive and you will need to include the dashes within the passcode, but not when entering the ISBN.

AAT

Q2022

Audit and Assurance

EXAM KIT

This Exam Kit supports study for the following AAT qualifications:
AAT Level 4 Diploma in Professional Accounting
AAT Diploma in Professional Accounting at SCQF Level 8

AAT: AUDIT AND ASSURANCE

British Library Cataloguing-in-Publication Data

A catalogue record for this book is available from the British Library.

Published by:

Kaplan Publishing UK

Unit 2 The Business Centre

Molly Millar's Lane

Wokingham

Berkshire

RG41 2QZ

ISBN: 978-1-83996-898-3

© Kaplan Financial Limited, 2024

Printed and bound in Great Britain.

The text in this material and any others made available by any Kaplan Group company does not amount to advice on a particular matter and should not be taken as such. No reliance should be placed on the content as the basis for any investment or other decision or in connection with any advice given to third parties. Please consult your appropriate professional adviser as necessary. Kaplan Publishing Limited and all other Kaplan group companies expressly disclaim all liability to any person in respect of any losses or other claims, whether direct, indirect, incidental, consequential or otherwise arising in relation to the use of such materials.

This Product includes content from the International Ethics Standards Board for Accountants (IESBA), published by the International Federation of Accountants (IFAC) in 2015 and is used with permission of IFAC.

This Product includes content from the International Auditing and Assurance Standards Board (IAASB), published by the International Federation of Accountants (IFAC) in 2015 and is used with permission of IFAC.

All rights reserved. No part of this examination may be reproduced or transmitted in any form or by any means, electronic or mechanical, including photocopying, recording, or by any information storage and retrieval system, without prior permission from Kaplan Publishing.

CONTENTS

	Page
Unit-specific information	P.4
Index to questions and answers	P.5
Exam technique	P.6
Kaplan's recommended revision approach	P.7

Practice Questions	1
Answers to Practice Questions	43
Mock assessment questions	81
Mock assessment answers	97

Features in this exam kit

In addition to providing a wide ranging bank of real exam style questions, we have also included in this kit:

- unit-specific information and advice on exam technique
- our recommended approach to make your revision for this particular unit as effective as possible.

You will find a wealth of other resources to help you with your studies on the AAT website:

www.aat.org.uk/

Quality and accuracy are of the utmost importance to us so if you spot an error in any of our products, please send an email to mykaplanreporting@kaplan.com with full details, or follow the link to the feedback form in MyKaplan.

Our Quality Co-ordinator will work with our technical team to verify the error and take action to ensure it is corrected in future editions.

KAPLAN PUBLISHING

UNIT-SPECIFIC INFORMATION

THE EXAM

FORMAT OF THE ASSESSMENT

The assessment for this unit consists of six compulsory, independent tasks. Included in the assessment are a number of extended writing requirements. Students will be assessed by computer-based assessment.

In any one assessment, students may not be assessed on all content, or on the full depth or breadth of a piece of content. The content assessed may change over time to ensure validity of assessment, but all assessment criteria will be tested over time.

The learning outcomes for this unit are as follows:

	Learning outcome	Weighting
1	Demonstrate an understanding of the audit and assurance framework	10%
2	Demonstrate the importance of professional ethics	15%
3	Evaluate the planning process for audit and assurance	25%
4	Evaluate procedures for obtaining sufficient and appropriate evidence	35%
5	Review and report findings	15%
	Total	100%

Time allowed

2 hours and 30 minutes

PASS MARK

The pass mark for all AAT CBAs is 70%.

 Always keep your eye on the clock and make sure you attempt all questions!

DETAILED SYLLABUS

The detailed syllabus and study guide written by the AAT can be found at:

www.aat.org.uk/

INDEX TO QUESTIONS AND ANSWERS

	Page Number	
	Questions	*Answers*
PRINCIPLES AND RESPONSIBILITIES		
Questions 1–34	1	43
SYSTEMS AND CONTROLS		
Questions 35–41	13	51
PLANNING, CONTROLLING AND RECORDING		
Questions 42–71	16	53
AUDIT TECHNIQUES		
Questions 72–101	25	62
COMPLETION AND REPORTING		
Questions 102–115	36	74

MOCK ASSESSMENT		
Questions and answers	81	97

EXAM TECHNIQUE

- **Do not skip any of the material** in the syllabus.

- **Read each question** *very* carefully.

- **Double-check your answer** before committing yourself to it.

- Answer **every** question – if you do not know an answer to a multiple choice question or true/false question, you don't lose anything by guessing. Think carefully before you **guess**.

- If you are answering a multiple-choice question, **eliminate first those answers that you know are wrong.** Then choose the most appropriate answer from those that are left.

- **Don't panic** if you realise you've answered a question incorrectly. Getting one question wrong will not mean the difference between passing and failing.

Computer-based exams – tips

- Do not attempt a CBA until you have **completed all study material** relating to it.

- On the AAT website there is a CBA demonstration. It is **ESSENTIAL** that you attempt this before your real CBA. You will become familiar with how to move around the CBA screens and the way that questions are formatted, increasing your confidence and speed in the actual exam.

- Be sure you understand how to use the **software** before you start the exam. If in doubt, ask the assessment centre staff to explain it to you.

- Questions are **displayed on the screen** and answers are entered using keyboard and mouse. At the end of the exam, you are given a certificate showing the result you have achieved.

- In addition to the traditional multiple-choice question type, CBAs will also contain **other types of questions**, such as number entry questions, drag and drop, true/false, pick lists or drop down menus or hybrids of these.

- In some CBAs you will have to type in complete computations or written answers.

- You need to be sure you **know how to answer questions** of this type before you sit the exam, through practice.

KAPLAN'S RECOMMENDED REVISION APPROACH

QUESTION PRACTICE IS THE KEY TO SUCCESS

Success in professional examinations relies upon you acquiring a firm grasp of the required knowledge at the tuition phase. In order to be able to do the questions, knowledge is essential.

However, the difference between success and failure often hinges on your exam technique on the day and making the most of the revision phase of your studies.

The **Kaplan Study Text** is the starting point, designed to provide the underpinning knowledge to tackle all questions. However, in the revision phase, poring over text books is not the answer.

Kaplan Pocket Notes are designed to help you quickly revise a topic area; however you then need to practise questions. There is a need to progress to exam style questions as soon as possible, and to tie your exam technique and technical knowledge together.

The importance of question practice cannot be over-emphasised.

The recommended approach below is designed by expert tutors in the field, in conjunction with their knowledge of the examiner and the specimen assessment.

You need to practise as many questions as possible in the time you have left.

OUR AIM

Our aim is to get you to the stage where you can attempt exam questions confidently, to time, in a closed book environment, with no supplementary help (i.e. to simulate the real examination experience).

Practising your exam technique is also vitally important for you to assess your progress and identify areas of weakness that may need more attention in the final run up to the examination.

In order to achieve this we recognise that initially you may feel the need to practice some questions with open book help.

Good exam technique is vital.

THE KAPLAN REVISION PLAN

Stage 1: Assess areas of strengths and weaknesses

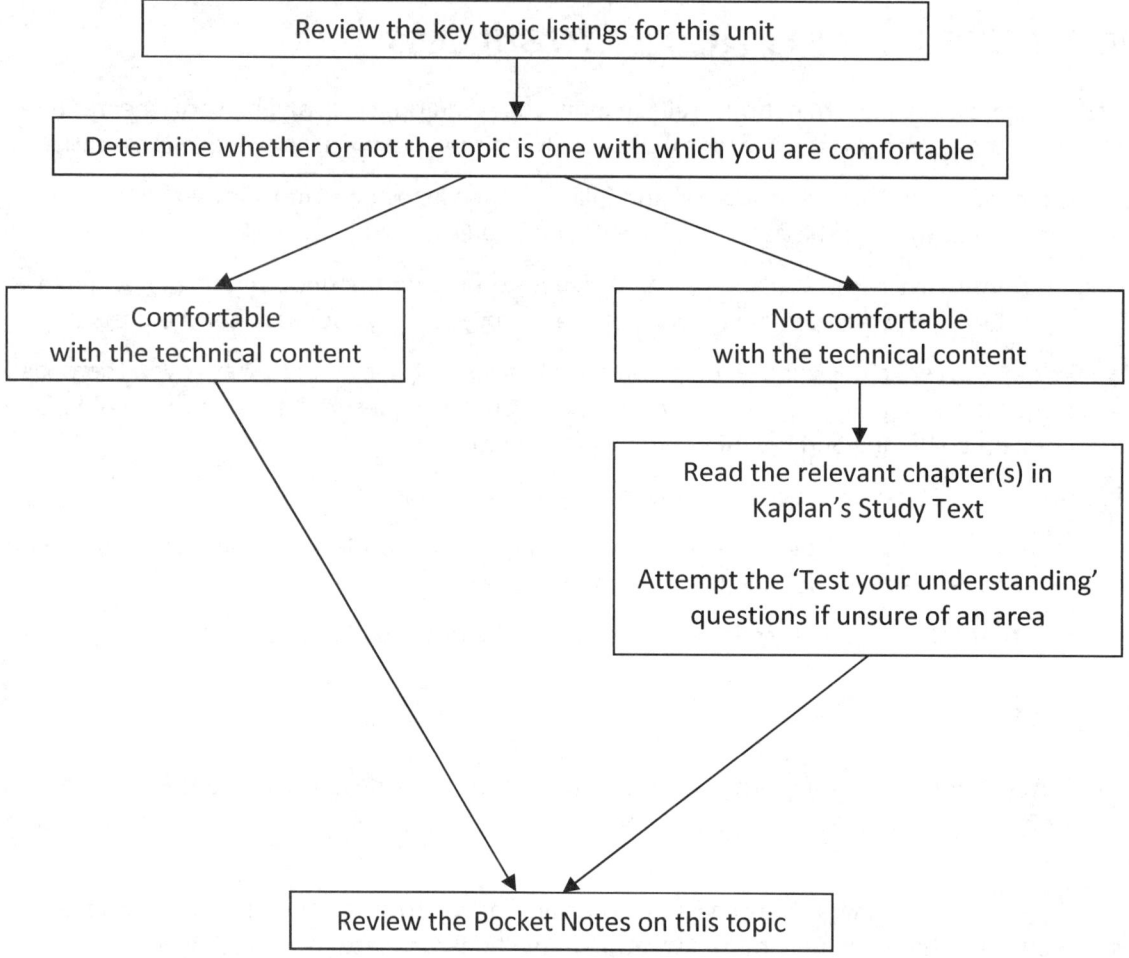

KAPLAN'S RECOMMENDED REVISION APPROACH

Stage 2: Practice questions

Follow the order of revision of topics as presented in this Kit and attempt the questions in the order suggested.

Try to avoid referring to Study Texts and your notes and the model answer until you have completed your attempt.

Review your attempt with the model answer and assess how much of the answer you achieved.

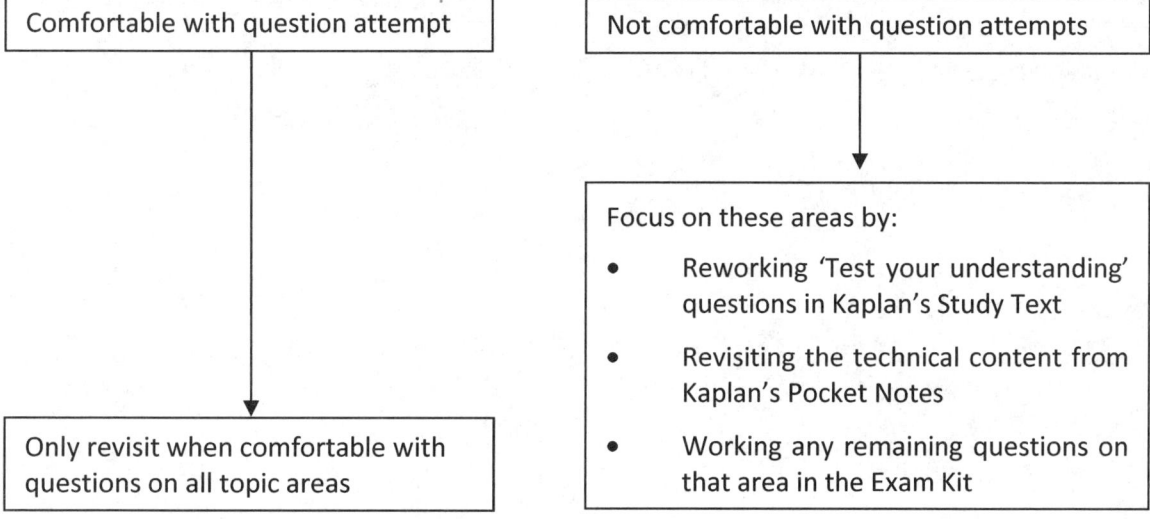

Stage 3: Final pre-exam revision

We recommend that you **attempt at least one mock examination** containing a set of previously unseen exam-standard questions.

Attempt the mock CBA online in timed, closed book conditions to simulate the real exam experience.

Section 1

PRACTICE QUESTIONS

PRINCIPLES AND RESPONSIBILITIES

1 **Complete the statement below on the overall objectives of the external auditor in conducting an audit of financial statements.**

The overall objectives of the external auditor are to obtain _____Gap 1_____ assurance about whether the financial statements are free from _____Gap 2_____ misstatement, whether due to fraud or error, thereby enabling the auditor to _____Gap 3_____ on whether the financial statements are prepared in all material respects in accordance with _____Gap 4_____.

Gap 1	✓
reasonable	
absolute	

Gap 2	✓
material	
all	

Gap 3	✓
express an opinion	
provide a guarantee	

Gap 4	✓
an applicable financial reporting framework	
International Standards on Auditing	

2 **Identify whether the following statements about audits are true or false.**

Statement	True ✓	False ✓
Auditors aim to give absolute assurance over the accuracy of the financial statements.		
A statutory audit gives reasonable assurance that the financial statements give a true and fair view.		

3 **Identify the level of assurance provided by the following extract from an auditor's report.**

In our opinion, the financial statements give a true and fair view of the financial position of the company as at 31 December 20X4.

Level of assurance	✓
Reasonable assurance	
Limited assurance	

KAPLAN PUBLISHING

4 Identify whether the following statements about professional scepticism are true or false.

Statement	True ✓	False ✓
The auditor must maintain professional scepticism throughout the duration of the audit.		
The client must maintain their professional scepticism throughout the duration of the audit.		

5 Identify whether the following statements about professional scepticism are true or false.

Statement	True ✓	False ✓
Professional scepticism refers to the auditor not believing anything the client says to them.		
Professional scepticism refers to the questioning mind the auditor should maintain.		

6 Complete the following statement on the respective responsibilities of the external auditor and management in conducting an audit of financial statements.

It is the responsibility of the _____Gap 1_____ to prepare the annual financial statements for the company and it is the responsibility of the _____Gap 2_____ to report to _____Gap 3_____ whether in their opinion the financial statements show a _____Gap 4_____.

Gap 1	✓
directors	
internal auditor	

Gap 2	✓
finance director	
external auditors	

Gap 3	✓
internal auditor	
shareholders	

Gap 4	✓
correct set of accounts	
true and fair view	

7 Complete the following statement on the key attributes required of the external auditor.

The most important professional attribute of an auditor is their _____Gap 1_____. This enables the auditor to _____Gap 2_____ as to the truth and fairness of the financial statements to the shareholders and gives assurance as to the _____Gap 3_____ of the auditor.

Gap 1	✓
experience	
independence	

Gap 2	✓
express an opinion	
provide a guarantee	

Gap 3	✓
reputation	
objectivity	

8 Identify whether the following statements about the external auditor are true or false.

Statement	True ✓	False ✓
The auditors are responsible for preparing the financial statements on which they report.		
The amounts in the financial statements are stated precisely.		
The external auditor provides reasonable assurance on the future viability of the audited entity.		

9 Identify whether the following statements about the International Auditing and Assurance Standards Board (IAASB) are true or false.

Statement	True ✓	False ✓
The IAASB works to improve the uniformity of auditing practices exclusively in the UK.		
The IAASB's standards contain basic principles and essential procedures together with related guidance in the form of explanatory and other material, including appendices.		

10 Identify which ONE of the following statements best describes the role of the International Auditing and Assurance Board (IAASB).

Statement	✓
The IAASB is responsible for setting auditing standards which are compulsory throughout the world.	
The IAASB is responsible for monitoring auditors to ensure that they comply with auditing standards.	
The IAASB is responsible for investigating and disciplining auditors who fail to comply with auditing standards.	
The IAASB is responsible for setting auditing standards which facilitate the convergence of national and international auditing standards.	

11 Identify which ONE of the following statements best describes the authority of International Standards on Auditing (ISAs) issued by the International Auditing and Assurance Board (IAASB).

Statement	✓
ISAs are best practice and can be followed by the auditor if they wish.	
ISAs are standards that compete with local standards and the auditor can choose which to use.	
ISAs are mandatory on all audits undertaken in the countries which have adopted ISAs unless the auditor has good reason for non-compliance.	
ISAs must be followed at all times and take precedence over Company Law of an individual country.	

12 Identify whether the following statements about the external auditor are true or false.

Statement	True ✓	False ✓
The primary duty of an auditor as set out in the Companies Act 2006 requires the auditor to report to the company's members on every set of accounts requiring statutory audit.		
The external auditor has a statutory duty to detect fraud as part of the main duties of the audit.		

13 Identify whether the following statements about auditor duties are true or false.

Statement	True ✓	False ✓
The external auditor has a common law duty of care towards certain third parties under the law of tort.		
The external auditor has a duty to exercise 'reasonable skill and care' to the client and any breach may lead to a claim of negligence by the client.		

PRACTICE QUESTIONS: SECTION 1

14 Identify whether the following statements are true or false.

Statement	True ✓	False ✓
Professional Indemnity Insurance is compulsory for all members of the Institute who have a practising certificate and are engaged in public practice, regardless of the amount of practice income.		
The external auditor has a duty to ensure quality management procedures are in place within the audit practice and are implemented by their personnel.		

15 Complete the following descriptions to identify the concepts they represent.

To comply with relevant laws and regulations and to avoid any action which discredits the profession. _____Gap 1_____

To ensure the auditor is far enough removed from the client to ensure that professional judgement can be in place. _____Gap 2_____

Gap 1	✓
Professional competence and due care	
Professional behaviour	

Gap 2	✓
Independence	
Objectivity	

16 Identify which ONE of the following situations is likely to give rise to a familiarity threat.

Situation	✓
Accepting a significant gift from an audit client.	
Owning shares in the client company.	
Acting as engagement partner of a listed audit client for more than 5 years.	

17 During the audit of Jesse Ltd, the audit senior discovered that the Managing Director, Morris, regularly pockets cash received from customers and does not include any details relating to the transaction in the accounting records of the business. Furthermore, none of this cash has been included as income on Morris's tax return.

Identify which ONE of the following is the appropriate action for the audit senior to take.

Action	✓
The matter should be reported to the tax authorities after discussion with Morris.	
The matter should be reported to the tax authorities without discussion with Morris.	
The matter should be reported to your firm's money laundering reporting officer after discussion with Morris.	
The matter should be reported to your firm's money laundering reporting officer without discussion with Morris.	

18 During the audit of Cayman Ltd, the audit senior discovered that during the year there was an issue of shares, all of which were bought by the Montego trust, based in the Bahamas. The audit senior made enquiries of the client as to the ownership and composition of this trust but was told that nobody except the Chairman knew anything about the trust. The Chairman is currently taking a 2 month holiday in the Bahamas.

Identify which ONE of the following is the appropriate action for the audit senior to take.

Action	✓
The matter should be reported to the CEO of Cayman Ltd immediately.	
The matter should be reported to the CEO of Cayman Ltd after discussions with the audit manager.	
The matter should be reported to the firm's money laundering officer after discussion with the CEO.	
The matter should be reported to the firm's money laundering officer without discussion with the CEO.	

19 Identify the ethical threat to independence posed by each of these situations.

Situation	Self-interest ✓	Self-review ✓	Familiarity ✓
Performance of internal and external audits of the same client.			
Overdue fees are outstanding from the client.			
The audit engagement partner and the Finance Director of the client are close friends.			

20 Below are statements regarding potential safeguards to be applied to protect an external auditor's independence and objectivity.

Identify whether each statement below is true or false.

Statement	True ✓	False ✓
When providing both internal and external audit services to a client, the assurance firm should use the same personnel for each of the assignments.		
The rotation of audit staff is an appropriate safeguard to mitigate a familiarity threat because the audit team has been in place for a number of years.		

PRACTICE QUESTIONS: SECTION 1

21 Below are statements regarding potential safeguards to be applied to protect an external auditor's independence and objectivity.

Identify whether the following statements are true or false.

Statement	True ✓	False ✓
Declining an opportunity to prepare a listed company's financial statements as well as doing the audit is an appropriate safeguard to the self-review threat.		
The rotation of audit staff is an appropriate safeguard to mitigate an advocacy threat when the auditor is representing the audit client in court.		

22 You are an Accounting Technician assisting in the audit of Sunnyside Ltd, an office stationery supplier, which has been an audit client for five years.

The Financial Controller of Sunnyside Ltd was absent during the year due to a family crisis. As the company had no suitable staff to fill the role, a qualified audit senior who worked part-time in your audit practice had also been given one day a week at Sunnyside Ltd for three months. She is now heading up the current audit of Sunnyside Ltd as the only audit senior. As a result of the Financial Controller only being part-time, additional audit time was required so the fee income from Sunnyside Ltd rose to 9% of your audit practice's total fees.

It comes to light during informal discussions that the Finance Director of Sunnyside Ltd knows the audit partner as they live round the corner from each other. Looking through social media feeds, you discover that they are also members of the same local golf club, regularly enjoying time with their families together round the swimming pool. You also notice that 25% of the audit fee from last year has not yet been paid and has not been chased for payment, in line with usual policy. There is a note in the records stating that an email was sent from the partner requesting that the fee is not chased.

Identify the ethical threat and action to be taken by the firm for each of the following situations.

Situation	Ethical threat	Action
The outstanding audit fee from last year.	Gap 1	Option 1
The total fee income from Sunnyside Ltd is 9% of the total fees for the audit practice.	Gap 2	Option 2
The partner and Finance Director know each other socially and have done for some time.	Gap 3	Option 3
The audit senior has been working as the Financial Controller of Sunnyside Ltd and is now leading the audit team.	Gap 4	Option 4

Gap 1	✓
Self-interest	
Intimidation	
Advocacy	
Self-review	

Option 1	✓
Do nothing	
Stop all audit work until payment is made	
Dismiss the partner	
Commence debt recovery process	

KAPLAN PUBLISHING

Gap 2	✓
Self-interest	
Intimidation	
Advocacy	
Familiarity	

Option 2	✓
Do nothing	
Resign from the audit	
As the fee was due to exceptional circumstances and will not reoccur do nothing	
Review whether independence is still met	

Gap 3	✓
Self-interest	
Self-review	
Advocacy	
Familiarity	

Option 3	✓
Do nothing	
Resign from the audit	
Rotate the partner from the audit	
Report the ethical threat to the audit committee	

Gap 4	✓
Self-interest	
Self-review	
Advocacy	
Intimidation	

Option 4	✓
Do nothing	
Remove the audit senior from the audit entirely	
Ensure audit senior does not work on areas she has prepared	
Report the ethical threat to the audit committee	

23   There are certain circumstances in which an external auditor must or may disclose confidential information relating to a client. Some circumstances require the client's permission, whilst others do not.

Identify whether the following circumstances require the external auditor to obtain the client's permission in order to disclose the information.

Circumstance	Requires the client's permission ✓	Does not require the client's permission ✓
The external auditor suspects that the client is involved in money laundering.		
The provision of evidence to support the external auditor in court.		
The provision of information as requested by the client's bank.		

PRACTICE QUESTIONS: SECTION 1

24 There are certain circumstances in which an external auditor must or may disclose confidential information relating to a client. Some circumstances require the client's permission, whilst others do not.

Identify whether the following circumstances require the external auditor to obtain the client's permission in order to disclose the information.

Circumstance	Requires the client's permission ✓	Does not require the client's permission ✓
A request to access the previous auditor's working papers in relation to a new client.		
The external auditor suspects that the client is involved in tax evasion.		
The external auditor suspects that a junior member of staff is involved in money laundering.		

25 The audit junior was overheard speaking to a friend in the pub after work one evening about the current audit the audit junior is working on.

The audit junior's friend works for a rival audit firm and they were discussing work that they had been involved in and the audit plan, approach to work and testing procedures.

Identify which TWO of the following would be appropriate action for the audit senior to take.

Action	✓
Report the audit junior to the client.	
Advise the audit junior they must keep all information about the client private.	
Invite the friend to join your audit firm.	
Ensure full training is given to your audit junior on client confidentiality and security of sensitive information.	
Make a formal complaint to the rival firm about the junior's friend.	

26 While working on the audit of Weed Ltd, the audit junior decided to take home some of the working papers to help gain a better understanding of the financial statements.

However, shortly after starting to review them a friend called around and started to look at the statements with the audit junior to give their own opinion.

The friend works for a rival audit firm and mentioned this to their audit senior at work the next day.

Identify which TWO of the following would be appropriate action for the audit senior to take.

Action	✓
Report the audit junior to the client.	
Advise the audit junior that no-one must be told about this.	
Ask the audit junior to disclose the fees being charged by their competitors.	
Ensure full training is given to your audit junior on client confidentiality and security of sensitive information.	

27 Identify which ONE of the following statements is correct in relation to the UK Corporate Governance Code (The Code).

Statement	✓
The Code is a set of statutory provisions.	
The Code, if broken, can give rise to civil liabilities.	
Should the Code be breached a fine will be imposed.	
The Code gives rise to disclosure requirements.	

28 Identify whether the following statements about corporate governance are true or false.

Statement	True ✓	False ✓
Corporate governance places reliance on the external auditor to ensure the company is run in the best interests of the shareholders.		
Corporate governance refers to how a company is directed and controlled.		
Good corporate governance practises may enhance the reputation of the company.		

29 Identify whether the following statements about internal audit are true or false.

Statement	True ✓	False ✓
Internal auditors can never be independent of those on which they are reporting, because they are employees of the company.		
The UK Corporate Governance Code requires all listed companies in the UK to have an internal audit function, unless the board explain to the shareholders why this decision has been made.		

30 Identify which of the following roles the internal auditors could carry out in respect of risk management and still operate effectively.

Role	Carry out ✓	Should not carry out ✓
Monitoring the company's overall risk strategy.		
Testing internal controls in the purchasing department.		
Designing a system of internal control in the production department.		

31 Identify whether the following statements about internal audit are true or false.

Statement	True ✓	False ✓
Internal auditors should not co-operate with external auditors.		
Statutory audits are carried out by external auditors only.		
The internal audit function forms part of the overall system of internal control.		

32 There are many similarities between the internal auditor and the external auditor but there are also some crucial differences to note. Identify whether the following statements relate to the internal auditor or the external auditor.

Statement	Internal auditor ✓	External auditor ✓
They provide an opinion on the financial statements.		
Their work is focussed on the operations of the entire business.		
The role can be carried out by employees of the entity.		
They are appointed by the shareholders of an entity.		

33 At present, Sistar Ltd does not have an internal audit function but the directors are establishing a team which will be responsible for a range of different internal audit assignments.

The board has started to compile a list of tasks for the internal audit department to carry out once it is up and running. It has been agreed that the first assignment to be completed will be for the internal auditors to review Sistar Ltd's processes over capital expenditure to verify if the right items are purchased at an appropriate time and competitive price.

Identify which type of internal audit assignment this represents.

Assignment	✓
A value for money audit	
A management audit	
A financial audit	

34 You are a member of the internal audit team of Snow Time Ltd, which operates an indoor snow centre for thrill-seekers to build up their confidence on a dry ski slope or a real snow slope before they venture off on holiday. Tickets can be purchased on the day using cash or a credit card or online in advance using a credit card. Tickets are valid for one day only and are all a standard price of £25 each. Tickets purchased in advance are offered at a reduced rate of 20% off the ticket price for a set date or 10% reduction for an open date ticket.

At the entrance, a limited number of booths are also available to purchase tickets with cash or credit card – manual tickets are issued, which are held in a locked cupboard in each booth. All sales are recorded on a till system showing the amount of each sale and the number of tickets issued.

As the work continues, you identify a number of unusual transactions.

Identify the action that should be taken with the following audit findings.

Findings	Action
The General Manager of Snow Time Ltd manned a booth during a period of staff illness and during this time a batch of tickets went missing.	PICKLIST
A member of staff in one of the booths has been selling tickets for the following day at a discount of 20%.	PICKLIST

Options
Do nothing
Refer to audit manager
Report to Snow Time Ltd management
Report to police

PRACTICE QUESTIONS: SECTION 1

SYSTEMS AND CONTROLS

35 When evaluating internal controls of an audit client, the external auditor needs to understand a number of technical terms.

Complete the following descriptions to identify the technical terms to which they relate.

The allocation of responsibilities within a process to different members of staff. _____Gap 1_____

The overall attitude of management about control and how important it is to the company. _____Gap 2_____

The part of the entity that performs activities designed to evaluate and improve internal controls and implement a risk management process. _____Gap 3_____

Gap 1	✓
Segregation of duties	
Risk assessment process	

Gap 2	✓
Collusion	
Control environment	

Gap 3	✓
Internal audit	
External audit	

36 When evaluating internal controls of an audit client, the external auditor needs to understand a number of technical terms.

Complete the following descriptions to identify the technical terms to which they relate.

The process of identifying the main issues facing a company. _____Gap 1_____

Members of staff acting together to defraud the company. _____Gap 2_____

Responsible for assessing internal controls to determine if reliance is going to be placed on them. _____Gap 3_____

Gap 1	✓
Segregation of duties	
Risk assessment process	

Gap 2	✓
Collusion	
Control environment	

Gap 3	✓
Internal audit	
External audit	

37 Match the following tests to the computer assisted audit technique from the picklist below.

Test	Computer assisted audit technique
Recalculation of the net book value of plant and machinery.	PICKLIST
Input of data with false dates to check the system identifies incorrect data for the period.	PICKLIST
Analysis of net profit by different product classifications.	PICKLIST

Options
Test data
Audit software
Data analytic tools

38 Match the following tests to the computer assisted audit technique from the picklist below.

Test	Computer assisted audit technique
To test that timesheets are not input for non-existent employees.	PICKLIST
Re-performance of addition or ageing of transactions.	PICKLIST
To discover patterns, deviations and inconsistencies within the population.	PICKLIST

Options
Test data
Audit software
Data analytic tools

39   Match the following tests to the computer assisted audit technique from the picklist below.

Test	Computer assisted audit technique
Comparison of the cost and net realisable value of inventory items to determine the lower value.	PICKLIST
Input of data with false inventory code numbers to check that the system rejects such data.	PICKLIST
Extraction of inventory balances over £5,000 in order to carry out further testing.	PICKLIST

Options
Test data
Audit software
Data analytic tools

40   Identify whether the following audit procedures will provide evidence that controls are operating as expected.

Procedure	True ✓	False ✓
Using test data to trace transactions from order to inclusion in the payables ledger.		
Walk through test of invoices being input into the system.		
Observation of staff processing invoices.		

41   Identify which ONE of the following financial statement assertions the auditor may find difficult to obtain sufficient audit evidence for if internal controls are not operating well.

Assertion	✓
Valuation	
Classification	
Completeness	
Occurrence	

AAT: AUDIT AND ASSURANCE

PLANNING, CONTROLLING AND RECORDING

42 As part of the planning process for the audit two clients, Blue Moon Ltd and Proud Pooches Ltd, the audit team carried out a series of analytical procedures on trade receivables and trade payables. These were conducted in order to identify the risk of material misstatement in the financial statements. The results of these analytical procedures are listed below.

Identify whether the results indicate that trade receivables and trade payables might have been under or overstated.

Results of analytical procedures	Understated ✓	Overstated ✓
The results of Blue Moon Ltd show that compared to the previous year trade receivables has increased by 30% and revenue has increased by 9%.		
The results of Blue Moon Ltd show that compared to the previous year trade payables has decreased by 15% and purchases have decreased by 10%.		
The results of Proud Pooches Ltd show that compared to the previous year trade receivables has increased by 20% and revenue has increased by 5%.		
The results of Proud Pooches Ltd show that compared to the previous year trade payables has decreased by 10% and purchases have decreased by 7%.		

43 Complete the following statement.

Audit risk is the risk that the auditor expresses an _____ opinion either on the financial statements as a whole or in relation to a particular financial area.

Options	✓
appropriate	
inappropriate	
acceptable	
unacceptable	

44 You are part way through the planning stage of the external audit of Frenchman Ltd. You are gathering information to understand the company's operations in order to reduce audit risk to an acceptable level.

Identify which of the following are components of the audit risk model.

Component	Yes ✓	No ✓
Inherent risk		
Control risk		
Identity risk		
Detection risk		

KAPLAN PUBLISHING

PRACTICE QUESTIONS: SECTION 1

45 Identify the component parts of audit risk being described by each of the following statements.

Statement	Component part
The risk that the audit procedures do not detect material misstatement in the financial statements.	PICKLIST
The risk that a client's internal controls have not detected a material misstatement.	PICKLIST
The risk of the auditor issuing an incorrect audit opinion.	PICKLIST
The risk of there being a material misstatement in the financial statements due to the nature of the client.	PICKLIST

Options
Inherent risk
Control risk
Detection risk
Audit risk

46 Identify whether the following actions would be likely to increase or decrease the control risk in relation to sales.

Action	Increase ✓	Decrease ✓
Sales invoices are only raised for goods that have been dispatched.		
No initial credit checks are made on new customers to gauge their creditworthiness.		
All customer receipts are correctly recorded.		

47 Identify whether the following will be likely to increase or decrease the reliability of a client's internal controls in affecting the risk of misstatement or fraud.

Action	Increase ✓	Decrease ✓
Due to cost saving measures, there is less segregation of duties amongst the payroll staff.		
The entity has recently introduced a new cash handling procedure with complete procedure notes distributed to all staff.		
Management regularly review budgets and compare to forecasts to analyse the company's performance.		

48 Identify whether the following statements about audit risk are true or false.

Statement	True ✓	False ✓
External auditors are able to control inherent risk and control risk so as to reduce audit risk to an acceptably low level.		
External auditors are able to control detection risk so as to reduce audit risk to an acceptably low level.		

49 Whilst planning the audit of Bluebean Ltd, you are required to consider how factors such as the entity's operating environment and its system of internal controls affect the risk of misstatement in the financial statements.

Identify whether the following factors are likely to increase, decrease, or have no effect on the risk of misstatement.

Factor	Increase ✓	Decrease ✓	No effect ✓
The entity is committed to employing personnel with appropriate accounting and financial reporting skills.			
The entity is to be sold and the purchase consideration will be determined as a multiple of reported profit.			
The entity's management does not intend to remedy deficiencies in internal controls identified by the external auditor.			

50 Identify which TWO of the following statements about materiality are true.

Statement	True ✓
As part of the audit planning, the auditor will determine the maximum amount of errors the auditor is willing to accept and still be satisfied that the financial statements show a true and fair view.	
Materiality is equally important to the auditor when expressing an opinion and the management when reviewing the financial statements.	
A material error in the financial statements may be described as the relative significance or importance of a particular matter in the context of the financial statements.	
A material error in the financial statements may be described as a lack of robust written processes and procedures in place to record each stage of a transaction.	

51 Identify which TWO of the following statements about materiality are true.

Statement	True ✓
Materiality is not capable of general mathematical definition as it has both qualitative and quantitative aspects.	
The auditor will consider a relatively small error in a month end procedure an indication of a potential material misstatement if that error is repeated each month.	
When determining materiality, the auditor just looks at the size of an item in comparison to the profit of the client.	
Auditing standards specify what percentage of profit would make an item material.	

52 Identify whether the following statements about audit planning are true or false.

Statement	True ✓	False ✓
Performance materiality is set a level above materiality as it only relates to the financial statements as a whole.		
The idea behind performance materiality is to reduce to an acceptably low level the probability that the aggregate uncorrected and undetected misstatements exceed materiality for the financial statements as a whole.		
Once established, performance materiality must not be changed as the audit progresses.		

53 Identify whether the following statements about audit planning are true or false.

Statement	True ✓	False ✓
Performance materiality should be set at a level below the level of materiality for the financial statements as a whole.		
Performance materiality is always a given percentage of overall materiality.		
All errors found, in excess of performance materiality, must be amended by the client in order to avoid the audit report being qualified.		

AAT: AUDIT AND ASSURANCE

54 You are planning the audit of Nectar Ltd, a new audit client which operates in the oil and gas exploration industry. During your planning meeting with the Finance Director, you were informed that the forecast profit before tax for this financial year is £9.5m based on revenues of £124m.

Identify which ONE of the following is the LEAST appropriate materiality level to be used in the audit of Nectar Ltd.

Materiality level	✓
£1.5 million	
£1.0 million	
£750,000	
£475,000	

55 You are the audit manager at Owl and Co responsible for the audit of Hawk Ltd.

The Finance Director has provided you with the most recent management accounts to enable you to perform preliminary analytical procedures. Using the information you have calculated the following ratios:

Ratio	Formula	Purpose	Current year	Prior year
Gross profit margin	$\dfrac{\text{Gross profit} \times 100}{\text{Revenue}}$	Profitability before taking overheads into account.	17%	26%
Payables payment period	$\dfrac{\text{Trade payables} \times 365}{\text{Credit purchases}}$	Average time taken to pay suppliers.	40 days	75 days
Receivables collection period	$\dfrac{\text{Trade receivables} \times 365}{\text{Credit revenue}}$	Average time taken to turn receivables into cash.	38 days	29 days

Identify which audit risks can be identified from the preliminary analytical procedures performed (Select ONE row).

Gross profit margin	Payables payment period	Receivables collection period	✓
Website sales may not be accurately recorded	Payables may not be accurately recorded	Extended credit terms may have been given to customers	
Revenue may have been recognised too early	Suppliers may be withdrawing credit terms	Receivables may not be completely recorded	
Revenue may not have occurred	Purchase invoices may have been recorded twice	Receivables may not exist	
Website sales may not be completely recorded	Payables may not be completely recorded	Receivables may be overvalued	

PRACTICE QUESTIONS: SECTION 1

56 Audit documentation serves a number of purposes.

Identify the purpose of each of the working papers in the table below by selecting the appropriate reason for preparation.

Working paper	Reason for preparation
Independence questionnaire completed by each member of the audit team.	PICKLIST
Copies of cash flow and profit forecasts and post year-end management accounts.	PICKLIST
Details of the review of assets in the factory whilst attending the inventory count.	PICKLIST

Options
Assess the going concern status
Compliance with independence and ethical requirements
Supporting valuation of assets

57 Identify whether the following statements about working papers are true or false.

Statement	True ✓	False ✓
Working papers must only be prepared in electronic form to ensure confidentiality and security.		
There are two main types of file for audit working papers; the permanent audit file and the current audit file.		
The date of the working papers and the name of the person preparing the file should be clearly stated on all documents.		

58 Identify whether the following statements about working papers are true or false.

Statement	True ✓	False ✓
The audit working papers are prepared and collated during the audit and should be retained in connection with the performance of the audit.		
The permanent audit file should not contain any copies of statutory or legal regulations or papers.		
The current audit file should include schedules showing the results of audit tests carried out.		

AAT: AUDIT AND ASSURANCE

59 Identify whether the following statements about working papers are true or false.

Statement	True ✓	False ✓
The auditor's working papers provide adequate evidence of the work that has been carried out and the conclusions reached contain sufficient appropriate audit evidence to support the conclusions made.		
The auditor will rely on a designated staff member from the client's workforce to assist in the compilation of the current audit file.		
The permanent audit files contain information of continuing importance to the audit such as board minutes of relevance, previous years' signed accounts, analytical reviews and engagement letters.		

60 Identify whether the following statements about working papers are true or false.

Statement	True ✓	False ✓
Working papers are prepared by the external auditor because there is a legal requirement to do so.		
The objective of working papers is to provide evidence that the audit was planned and performed in accordance with International Standards on Auditing.		
Working papers should contain the name of who performed the audit work and the date it was performed.		

61 Identify which ONE of the following statements about working papers is true.

Statement	True ✓
The detailed content of each type of audit working paper is strictly detailed in the ISAs.	
The primary objective of working papers is to prove to the audit partner that the work was done.	
Working papers should clearly state which year-end they pertain to and show evidence that they have been reviewed.	

62 You are planning the audit of Top Notch Ltd (Top Notch), a chain of hairdressing salons in the Midlands.

Top Notch employs 40 staff throughout the region. The majority of staff are paid weekly via BACs transfer. However, a small number of casual weekend staff are paid cash in hand on a weekly basis.

Approximately half of Top Notch's customers pay by credit or debit card, with the remainder paying in cash. Cash is banked weekly by the Salon Manager and a note is sent to Head Office with the amount banked. No other checks of the tills are carried out.

22 KAPLAN PUBLISHING

Each salon purchases its own goods (shampoo, conditioner etc.) from local suppliers. Invoices are sent directly to Head Office, without any check by the individual salon. Any larger capital purchases must be authorised by Head Office.

Discuss the audit risks, from the scenario above, that should be considered when planning the audit of Top Notch Ltd. Where possible, your answer should refer to specific items in the financial statements which may be at risk of misstatement.

63   You are planning the audit of Florida Air Conditioning (FAC).

FAC is a privately owned business, run by two brothers. The company was set up in 2001 and has been very successful and now employs 60 staff.

FAC has two income streams:

- sale of air conditioning units, and
- provision of air conditioning service support contracts (vary from 1 – 3 years).

Customers are invoiced after installation of air conditioning units. Customers are invoiced annually in advance for service support contracts.

FAC manufactures its air conditioning units in house. FAC's inventory consists of finished units, part finished units (work in progress) and component parts used for the production of units and spares for the service contracts. FAC sources some of the component parts for its units from an overseas supplier and must pay these invoices in the supplier's local currency.

FAC offers a 1 year warranty on all new purchases of air conditioning units. The company has included a warranty provision on the statement of financial position and it is material to the financial statements.

Discuss the audit risks, from the scenario above, that should be considered when planning the audit of Florida Air Conditioning. Where possible, your answer should refer to specific items in the financial statements which may be at risk of misstatement.

64   During the year ended 31 December 20X2, Green Ltd took out a bank loan of £1 million to fund a capital project. The terms of the loan require:

- Capital repayments, over 5 years, in monthly instalments commencing 1 July 20X2.
- Interest at 9% per annum payable monthly.
- Profit before interest and tax in the monthly management accounts to cover interest at least four times.

Set out, in a manner suitable for inclusion in the audit plan the audit risks relating to the loan.

65   During the year ended 31 December 20X2, Pepco Ltd acquired a fleet of 10 new lorries for distribution, at a cost of £7m, payable in 3 annual instalments on a finance agreement at 8%.

Set out, in a manner suitable for inclusion in the audit plan the audit risks relating to the finance agreement and related non-current assets.

66   Tileclose Ltd is a civil engineering company that provides a pipe-laying service to the energy, water and telecommunications industries. It uses much heavy plant and machinery, and is subject to the strict provisions of Health and Safety at work regulations.

Set out, in a manner suitable for inclusion in the audit plan the audit risks relating to Tileclose Ltd.

AAT: AUDIT AND ASSURANCE

67 You are an Accounting Technician assisting in the audit of Fallowfield Ltd, a manufacturer of washing machines, for the year ended 31 May 20X3. Historically, all washing machines were sold with a two-year warranty against defective materials and workmanship. In June 20X2, Fallowfield increased the warranty period to five years to match the warranties offered by its competitors. Fallowfield includes a provision for such warranties in its financial statements. The provision is based on the finance director's assessment of future claims.

You have been provided with the following relevant extracts from the financial statements:

	20X3 (draft) £000	20X2 £000
Revenue	28,990	25,260
Non-current provision for warranty claims	289	253
Current provision for warranty claims	319	316

Explain the factors which could indicate that the provision for warranty claims may be materially misstated.

68 You are an Accounting Technician assisting in the audit of Salamander Ltd. You are planning the audit for the year ended 31 March 20X3. The engagement partner has identified payroll as a key area of audit risk. Salamander Ltd's employees work in ten different offices across Europe and the total workforce has grown by 8% during the year ended 31 March 20X3. On 1 April 20X2, Salamander Ltd awarded a company-wide pay increase of 3%.

List the analytical procedures, relevant to payroll, to be included in your audit plan.

69 You are part of the audit team for the external audit of Anker Ltd for the year ended 31 December 20X2. At the planning meeting with the finance director or Anker Ltd, you ascertained that payroll processing, which had been outsourced for a number of years, was brought back in house in October 20X2.

Management was not satisfied with the performance of the service provider and terminated the contract. The service provider had been responsible for making payments to the employees and the monthly remittances to HMRC. Two of Anker Ltd's finance team members have been trained in payroll processing.

Discuss the audit risks, from the scenario above, that should be considered when planning the audit of Anker Ltd.

70 You are an Accounting Technician assisting in the audit of Derrick Ltd for the year ended 31 December 20X3. The following extracts are from the draft financial statements of Derrick Ltd:

You have been provided with the following relevant extracts from the financial statements:

	20X3 (draft) £000	20X2 (actual) £000
Extract from statement of profit or loss		
Loss on sale of plant	(550)	–
Depreciation charge for the year	(480)	(858)
Extract from statement of financial position		
Non-current assets		
Property, plant and equipment	4,265	3,889

On 1 January 20X2, freehold land was revalued by £1,000,000 and £850,000 was received from the sale of plant. Derrick Ltd also made additions of £1,066,000 to property plant and equipment during the year. All amounts are material to the financial statements of Derrick Ltd.

Identify the risks of misstatement in the financial statements of Derrick Ltd for the year ended 31 December 20X3 in respect of the audit of property, plant and equipment.

71 You are part of the audit team for the external audit of Aldo Ltd for the year ended 31 May 20X3. Aldo Ltd's principal activity is the hiring out of transport to the TV/ film industry. The company commenced trading on 1 June 20X2 and, although the company's revenue and assets are below the thresholds for statutory audit purposes, the company's bank requires the financial statements to be subject to a full audit. Your initial enquiries reveal that a computer package is used to maintain the accounting records and that these records are maintained by a part-qualified accountant who is helped by a part-time payroll clerk.

State, with reasons, an appropriate approach to the audit of Aldo Ltd, which addresses the extent of tests of controls and substantive procedures, including analytical procedures.

AUDIT TECHNIQUES

72 **Identify whether the following procedures are a test of control, test of detail or an analytical procedure.**

Procedure	Test of control ✓	Test of detail ✓	Analytical procedure ✓
Developing an expectation of payroll costs by taking into account last year's payroll figure, annual pay rises and starters and leavers.			
Reviewing purchase orders to see if they have been approved by a relevant member of staff.			
Recalculating PAYE and NIC costs for payroll.			
Calculating receivables and payables days and comparing to the prior year.			
Reviewing bank reconciliations to ensure they have been prepared and reviewed by an appropriate person.			

73 You are an audit junior gathering evidence on the audit of Remy Ltd. You have been asked by your manager to conduct verification techniques in respect of sales and receivables, more specifically to inspect sales invoices. You will gain assurance about different assertions depending on the information on the invoice.

In respect of the information below, identify the assertion for which that information will provide assurance.

Information	Accuracy ✓	Classification ✓	Existence ✓
Receivables circularisation letter			
After date receipts			
Description of goods			

74 You are an audit junior gathering evidence on the audit of Chiltern Ltd. You have been asked by your manager to conduct verification techniques in respect of purchases. As part of this assignment you will carry out the audit tests to confirm existence, valuation or completeness.

In respect of the information below, identify the assertion for which that information will provide assurance.

Information	Valuation ✓	Completeness ✓	Existence ✓
The auditor seeks assurance that the asset or liability is recorded at the correct value.			
A full inventory check is performed with the auditor verifying inventory sheets to inventory on shelves.			

75 As part of verification techniques in respect of purchases, an auditor will inspect purchase invoices. The auditor will gain assurance about different assertions depending on the information on the invoice.

In respect of the information below, identify the assertion for which that information will provide assurance.

Information	Assertion
Date of the invoice	PICKLIST
Description of the item purchased	PICKLIST
Monetary amount	PICKLIST
Addressee of the invoice	PICKLIST

Options
Accuracy
Classification
Cut-off
Existence
Rights and obligations

76 **Complete the following descriptions to identify the technical terms to which they relate.**

A sampling approach whereby items are chosen in a sequential order. _____Gap 1_____

A sampling approach whereby items are selected with a constant interval between selections. _____Gap 2_____

The risk that the auditor misinterprets the audit evidence obtained. _____Gap 3_____

Gap 1	✓
Block sampling	
Stratification	

Gap 2	✓
Haphazard sampling	
Systematic sampling	

Gap 3	✓
Sampling risk	
Non-sampling risk	

77 When selecting items in order to perform tests of detail, the external auditor has to consider a number of factors.

Identify whether the following factors will result in an increase in sample size, a decrease in sample size or have a negligible effect on sample size.

Factor	Increase ✓	Decrease ✓	No effect ✓
Being able to test very easily 90% of the sales invoices by way of a proof in total.			
Internal controls are found to be weak and not operating effectively.			
The audit client requesting that the auditor reduces the amount of testing.			

78 The external auditor may adopt an audit approach which involves undertaking either:

- tests of controls and substantive procedures, or
- substantive procedures only, with no tests of controls.

Identify the most likely approach to be adopted by the external auditor in each of the following circumstances.

Circumstance	Tests of controls and substantive procedures ✓	Substantive procedures only, with no tests of controls ✓
The audited entity was only set up a year ago, and there is only one member of staff in the accounting department.		
There is no segregation of duties within the accounting department of the client.		
The client has an internal audit department which reviews controls throughout the year.		

79 Identify the most likely approach to be adopted by the external auditor in each of the following circumstances.

Circumstance	Tests of controls and substantive procedures ✓	Substantive procedures only, with no tests of controls ✓
The entity has a strong control environment.		
A large fraud has been identified which came about due to the collusion of several members of staff.		
A new accounting package was introduced at the beginning of the year and there have been significant operational deficiencies with the new system.		

PRACTICE QUESTIONS: SECTION 1

80 You are undertaking the external audit of Green Garden Ltd, a company which manufactures and sells high quality garden furniture. You will be using tests of controls and substantive procedures to gather audit evidence.

For each of the procedures listed below, identify whether it is a test of control or a substantive procedure.

Procedure	Test of control ✓	Substantive procedure ✓
Perform tests on the supplier statement reconciliation process to confirm the completeness of payables.		
Reviewing credit control procedures for recoverability of receivables.		

81 Auditors use tests of controls and substantive procedures to gather audit evidence.

For each of the procedures listed below, identify whether it is a test of control or a substantive procedure.

Procedure	Test of control ✓	Substantive procedure ✓
Comparison of the current year's revenue figure with the previous year's figure.		
Observation of the despatch procedures in respect of goods leaving an entity's warehouse.		
Vouching of an addition to non-current assets to the supplier's invoice.		

82 When carrying out the audit of Beach Ltd, the audit junior has carried out the bank reconciliation process for a sample month and has noticed a number of transactions for cash withdrawals that have no supporting documentation.

The manager informed the audit junior that this type of transaction was necessary for the day to day running of the business and not everyone could remember to obtain receipts or supporting documentation.

The value of the withdrawals has increased significantly throughout the period and the audit junior believes it may be significant in the financial statements.

In respect of this matter, identify the appropriate response.

No further action ✓	Refer to supervisor ✓

83 When carrying out the audit of Sunshine Ltd, the audit junior has documented an invoice for the cost of a family holiday for the Managing Director.

The payables ledger clerk informed the audit junior that this type of invoice is received on a regular basis with the instruction to include the costs in general expenses.

The value of the invoice for the holiday is immaterial in terms of key figures in the financial statements.

In respect of this matter, identify the appropriate response.

No further action	Refer to supervisor
✓	✓

84 During the external audit of Prep Ltd, the audit junior identified an invoice for the cost of school fees for the Managing Director's children. The payables ledger clerk informed the audit junior that the Managing Director had told her to hide the costs in sundries. The amount of the school fees is insignificant in terms of key figures in the financial statements.

In respect of this matter, identify the appropriate response.

No further action	Refer to supervisor
✓	✓

85 During the external audit of Dodge Ltd, the audit junior identified a number of occurrences where mileage claims were processed through the payroll for staff that did not appear on the approved mileage list supplied by the payroll manager.

The ledger clerk said that there were valid reasons for these expenses but could not give any specifics.

The values were not of a material nature and discussions with the payroll manager indicated that systems had been put in place to eliminate this in the future.

In respect of this matter, identify the appropriate response.

No further action	Refer to supervisor
✓	✓

86 During the external audit of Silk Ltd, the audit junior identified two instances where a number of time sheets were not signed by the Payroll Manager prior to being processed through the monthly pay process and posting to the ledger. Both instances occurred when the payroll supervisor who is responsible for verifying the documents was on annual leave. Subsequent further tests indicated no similar weakness following the supervisor's return to work.

In respect of this matter, identify the appropriate response.

No further action	Refer to supervisor
✓	✓

PRACTICE QUESTIONS: SECTION 1

87 During the external audit of Trike Ltd, the audit junior identified a number of occurrences where the financial data entered into the computer spreadsheets was incorrectly input, with some of the errors causing material differences in the financial statements.

The junior has also noted that there is no virus protection on the computers used to generate the financial statements and that staff regularly use this computer to download games, and log onto social networking sites.

In respect of this matter, identify the appropriate response.

No further action	Refer to supervisor
✓	✓

88 During the external audit of Jemima Ltd, the audit junior identified two instances of failure to authorise purchase invoices prior to posting to the payables ledger. Both instances occurred when the purchase supervisor who is responsible for authorising such transactions was away on sick leave, and further tests indicated no similar failings following her return to work.

In respect of this matter, identify the appropriate response.

No further action	Refer to supervisor
✓	✓

89 During the external audit of Perch Ltd, the audit junior was requested to add up ten pages of the cash book from throughout the year. Nine of the pages added up correctly but one page had a transposition error leading to it being under cast by £69.

The turnover of Perch Ltd was £3.5m for the year and the profit was £469,000.

In respect of this matter, identify the appropriate response.

No further action	Refer to supervisor
✓	✓

90 Smart Sense Ltd is a small company which undertakes the installation and upgrade of computer software under short-term fixed-price contracts.

All direct costs incurred that relate to each contract are recorded in the company's job costing system which is fully integrated with the purchases and payroll applications.

The Financial Controller uses the job costing records to estimate the value of work in progress for the monthly management accounts and the year-end financial statements.

Set out, in a manner suitable for inclusion in the audit plan, the audit procedures to be undertaken in order to ensure that work in progress is fairly stated in the financial statements.

91 During the audit of Short Circuit Ltd, a computer manufacturing company, the audit junior asks how it is possible to establish the existence, completeness and ownership of the company's non-current assets.

Set out, in a manner suitable for inclusion in the audit plan, the audit procedures to be undertaken in order to gather evidence to support these issues and ensure the assets are fairly stated in the financial statements.

92 Honeysuckle Ltd is a company which hires out various items of equipment to a range of customers ranging from small contractors to very large building companies. The hire periods range from one day to six months and there is a great variety in the number of items hired at any one time per customer. For individual items and hire periods of less than one month, Honeysuckle Ltd issues an invoice on completion of the hire period. For hire periods greater than one month a progress invoice is issued at each month end. The credit period is 30 days.

Set out, in a manner suitable for inclusion in the audit plan, the audit procedures to be undertaken in order to ensure that receivables are fairly stated in the financial statements.

93 You are a member of the internal audit team for Funfit Gyms, who own exclusive gyms in the UK. The audit manager has provided you with a copy of the procedure notes issued to gym reception staff.

- Day bookings can be made for gym visits only over the internet or by phone. Payment for day visits are made on entry to the gym and can be by cash or card.

- Products such as towels, water bottles and sports equipment can be purchased from reception and must be paid for by cash or card on purchase.

- The receptionist records all product sales and payments for day bookings on a spreadsheet created and maintained by the accountant. This is saved on a shared drive so they both have access.

- Selected products are displayed in a cabinet alongside the reception desk. Additional items are kept behind the desk in a secure cupboard and the key is held in the cash box. When purchases are made, the credit card receipt or cash is placed in the cash box. The key to the cash box is lying on display on top of the reception desk.

- The contents of the cash box are taken by the receptionist on duty to the accountant's office by 17:30 each weekday. When reception is closed, it is the responsibility of the head receptionist to secure the cash box in the safe inside the General Manager's office.

You are preparing a summary for the audit plan in which you should:

(i) **determine the audit approach to testing based on current procedures at Funfit Gyms.**

(ii) **identify FOUR control procedures that could be implemented to mitigate areas of concern identified in part (i).**

94 You are a member of the audit team for a company which uses one of its properties to operate a car park. The car park operates as follows:

Operating details

All cars enter past an automatic barrier and machine which issues a date and time-stamped entry ticket to the car driver. All cars to leave through one manned exit barrier.

When cars leave, duration of stay and fee are calculated and entered by the staff member on the pre-numbered ticket issued by the ticket machine. The correct fee is received by the attendant, who retains the pre-numbered ticket.

At the end of the day, all cash received is banked. During the afternoon a member of accounts department staff from head office collects all used tickets and records of cash banked. All accounting records are maintained at head office.

(i) **Describe TWO tests of controls you would perform to ensure that revenue is complete.**

(ii) **Explain what is meant by the term 'test of control'.**

95 You are a member of the audit team for the FireFly Tennis Club. Under the rules of the club, the annual accounts must be audited by an independent auditor. The club's year end is 30 September. The club owns 12 tennis courts and members pay an annual fee to use the courts and participate in club championships. The club had 430 members as at 1 October 2021.

Revenue is derived from membership fees. Each member pays a fee of £400 per annum. Fees for the new financial year are payable within one month of the club year end. Approximately 10% of members do not renew their membership. New members joining during the year pay 50% of the total fees that would have been payable had they been members for a full year. During 2022, 50 new members joined the club. No members pay their fees before they are due.

Main items of expenditure are court maintenance, power for floodlights and tennis balls.

The treasurer pays for all expenditure using the club's debit card. Receipts are obtained for all expenses and these are filed in date order. The treasurer also prepares the annual financial statements. The date is now 16 December 2022 and the treasurer has just prepared the financial statements to be audited.

(i) **Describe the audit procedures that should be undertaken to test the completeness of revenue for the FireFly Tennis Club.**

(ii) **Describe the audit procedures that should be undertaken to test the completeness and accuracy of expenditure for the FireFly Tennis Club.**

96 Porthos, a limited liability company, is a reseller of sports equipment, specialising in racquet sports such as tennis, squash and badminton. The company purchases equipment from a variety of different suppliers and then resells it online as the only selling media. The company has over 150 different types of racquets available in inventory, each identified via a unique product code.

Customers place their orders directly on the website. Most orders are for one or two racquets only. The ordering/sales software automatically verifies the order details, customer address and credit card information prior to orders being verified and goods being despatched. The integrity of the ordering system is checked regularly by ArcherWeb, an independent internet service company.

You are a member of the external audit team of Porthos, and you have just started planning the audit of the revenue system of the company. You have decided to use test data to check the input of details into the revenue system. This will involve entering dummy orders into the Porthos system from an online terminal.

AAT: AUDIT AND ASSURANCE

(i) **List the test data you will use in your audit of the financial statements of Porthos to confirm the completeness and accuracy of input into the revenue system, explaining the reason for each item of data.**

You are also considering using audit software as part of your substantive testing of the data files in the revenue and inventory systems of Porthos.

(ii) **Briefly explain some of the difficulties of using audit software**

(iii) **List the audit tests that you can program into your audit software for the revenue and inventory system in Porthos, explaining the reason for each test.**

97   DinZee Co assembles fridges, microwaves, washing machines and other similar domestic appliances from parts procured from a large number of suppliers. You are attending their inventory count. On the day of the inventory count, you attended depot nine at DinZee. You observed the following activities:

1   Prenumbered count sheets were being issued to client's staff carrying out the count. The count sheets showed the inventory records for checking against physical stock.

2   All count staff were drawn from the inventory warehouse and were counting in teams of two.

3   Three counting teams were allocated to each area of the stores to count, although the teams were allowed to decide which pair of staff counted which inventory within each area. Staff were warned that they had to remember which inventory had been counted.

4   Information was recorded on the count sheets in pencil so amendments could be made easily as required.

5   Any inventory not located on the pre-numbered inventory sheets was recorded on separate inventory sheets – which were numbered by staff as they were used.

6   At the end of the count, all count sheets were collected and the numeric sequence of the sheets checked; the sheets were not signed.

(a) **List the deficiencies in the system for counting inventory at depot nine. For each deficiency, explain why it is a deficiency and state how it can be overcome.**

(b) (i) **State the aim of a test of control and the aim of a substantive procedure.**

(ii) **In respect of your attendance at Dinzee Co's inventory count, state one test of control and one substantive procedure that you should perform.**

98   Your firm has recently been appointed as auditors to Green Co, a gardening equipment manufacturer. In the course of enquiries, your audit manager was informed that the company sold only on credit terms and that it had incurred several material irrecoverable debts during the year. These had occurred due to fundamental weaknesses in the sales and trade receivables system.

Explain FIVE substantive procedures that your firm could carry out to verify the irrecoverable debts figure as reported in the financial statements of Green Co.

PRACTICE QUESTIONS: SECTION 1

99 Your firm has recently been appointed auditor of Andrew Manufacturing Co, and you have been asked to carry out the audit of non-current assets at the company's year-end of 30 September 20X3.

The company operates from its own premises, and the draft financial statements show the following movement on non-current assets for the year.

	Buildings £	Plant and equipment £	Motor vehicles £	Total £
Cost:				
At 1 October 20X2	162,577	46,003	20,175	228,755
Additions	2,534	8,721	7,500	18,755
Disposals	–	(5,937)	(5,250)	(11,187)
At 30 September 20X3	165,111	48,787	22,425	236,323
Depreciation:				
At 1 October 20X2	2,104	20,059	10,353	32,516
Charge for the year	1,102	4,878	5,741	11,721
On disposals	–	(4,808)	(3,937)	(8,745)
At 30 September 20X3	3,206	20,129	12,157	35,492

It is the company's policy to charge a full year's depreciation in the year of acquisition and nothing in the year of disposal.

The company's accounting policies are to provide depreciation at the following rates:

Buildings	4% on cost
Plant and equipment	10% on cost
Motor vehicles	25% on cost

The company maintains a non-current asset register for plant and equipment and motor vehicles.

Explain FIVE substantive procedures that your firm could carry out to verify the non-current assets figure as reported in the financial statements of for the year ended 30 September 20X3.

100 Your audit client, Pear Co, is a long established building renovations company and prepares its annual financial statements to 30 April. The financial statements for the year ended 30 April 20X3 revealed the following item, together with comparative for the previous year.

Item	30 April 20X3 £	30 April 20X2 £
Trade payables	315,000	205,200

Pear Co's reported pre-tax profit for the year ended 30 April 20X3 was £990,000.

Explain FIVE substantive procedures that the auditor of Pear Co could carry out to test the completeness and valuation assertions for trade payables.

101 Your audit client, Apple Co, is a national construction company and prepares its annual financial statements to 30 June. The financial statements for the year ended 30 June 20X3 revealed the following item, together with comparative for the previous year.

Item	30 June 20X3 £	30 June 20X2 £
Provision	81,000	–

The provision of £81,000 relates to a legal obligation to carry out repairs to a public building damaged by employees of Apple when renovating an adjoining building. Apple Co's reported pre-tax profit for the year ended 30 June 20X3 was £990,000.

Explain FIVE substantive procedures that the auditor of Apple Co should carry out to verify the completeness and valuation assertions of the provision balance.

COMPLETION AND REPORTING

102 You are undertaking the external audit of Crescent Ltd, which imports organic tea leaves to the UK. Over the past few years they have seen increasing competition and as a result, demand for their products has decreased. The profit before tax for the year was £865,600 (£994,400 in the previous year).

The audit review includes an assessment of uncorrected misstatements, which identified a number of transactions.

Assess the following uncorrected misstatements for materiality.

Uncorrected misstatement	Material	
		✓
Expenses payments to staff of £21,600 not authorised.	Yes	
	No	
Errors in recording returned products resulting in overstatement of sales totalling £89,923.	Yes	
	No	

103 It is 1 July 20X1. You are the manager responsible for the audit of Greenfields Ltd and you are performing the final review of the audit for the year ended 31 March 20X1. Greenfields Ltd specialises in manufacturing equipment which can help to reduce toxic emissions in the production of chemicals. The company has grown rapidly over the past eight years and this is due partly to the warranties that the company gives to its customers. It guarantees its products for five years and if problems arise in this period it undertakes to fix them, or provide a replacement product. The following issues have been left for your attention.

Receivable balance owing from Yellowmix Ltd

Greenfields Ltd has a material receivable balance owing from its customer, Yellowmix Ltd. During the year-end audit, your team reviewed the ageing of this balance and found that no payments had been received from Yellowmix Ltd for over six months, and Greenfields Ltd would not allow this balance to be circularised. Instead management has assured your team that they will provide a written representation confirming that the balance is recoverable.

Warranty provision

The warranty provision included within the statement of financial position is material. The audit team has performed testing over the calculations and assumptions which are consistent with prior years. The team has requested a written representation from management confirming the basis and amount of the provision are reasonable.

Complete the statements below about written representations.

A written representation _____Gap 1_____ in respect of the receivable balance. This is because _____Gap 2_____.

A written representation _____Gap 3_____ in respect of the warranty provision. This is because _____Gap 4_____.

Gap 1	✓
is appropriate	
is not appropriate	

Gap 2	✓
The matter involves management judgement	
Other procedures can be performed which provide more reliable evidence	

Gap 3	✓
is appropriate	
is not appropriate	

Gap 4	✓
The matter involves management judgement	
Other procedures can be performed which provide more reliable evidence	

104 During the audit of Pump Ltd, it was discovered that although the company maintains a non-current asset register to record the details of its sports and fitness equipment, no checking procedures other than reconciliation with the nominal ledger are undertaken.

Prepare extracts, suitable for inclusion in a report to management of Pump Ltd, which sets out:

(i) the possible consequences of the deficiencies

(ii) the recommendations you would make.

105 Delta Ltd's sales invoices are produced by its computer system using the relevant price held as standing data on the sales master file. Selling prices are updated by the receivables ledger clerk on the verbal authority of the Sales Director.

Prepare extracts, suitable for inclusion in a report to management of Delta Ltd, which sets out:

(i) the possible consequences of the deficiencies

(ii) the recommendations you would make.

106 During the audit of Pharo Ltd, a manufacturing company, it was discovered that when goods other than raw materials arrive to the warehouse door, a member of the warehouse staff sends an email to the person they think the goods were intended for to ask them to come to the warehouse to pick them up. No other action is taken.

Prepare extracts, suitable for inclusion in a report to management of Pharo Ltd, which sets out:

(i) the possible consequences of the deficiencies

(ii) the recommendations you would make.

107 You are part of a team auditing the financial statements of Smartbuy Co. The company sells home decorating and maintenance products from a large retail and warehouse unit.

From enquiries into the company's systems of internal control you have ascertained the following information:

Inventory purchases

New inventory is ordered over the telephone by the company buyer. The buyer maintains a record of telephone orders. When goods are subsequently received, the buyer has sole responsibility for checking goods received for quantity only, to the record of telephone orders. Invoices from suppliers are sent to the buyer for authorisation, before being forwarded to the Accounts Department for entry into the accounting records and subsequent payment.

Prepare extracts, suitable for inclusion in a report to management of Smartbuy Co, which sets out:

(i) THREE deficiencies in the system

(ii) the possible consequences of the deficiencies

(iii) the recommendations you would make.

108 The following statements detail opinions given by the auditor on the financial statements of two companies.

Identify whether the audit opinions detail a qualified opinion, unmodified opinion or disclaimer of opinion dependent on the statement.

Statement	Qualified opinion ✓	Unmodified opinion ✓	Disclaimer of opinion ✓
In our opinion: The financial statements give a true and fair view, in accordance with UK Generally Accepted Accounting Practice, of the state of the company's affairs as at 31 March 2008 and of its profit for the year then ended. The financial statements have been properly prepared in accordance with the Companies Act 2006; and the information given in the Directors' Report is consistent with the financial statements.			
Extract: I planned my audit so as to obtain all the information and explanations which I considered necessary in order to provide me with sufficient evidence to give reasonable assurance that the financial statements are free from material misstatements. In forming my opinion I also evaluated the overall adequacy of the presentation of information in the financial statements. However, the evidence available to me was limited by the fundamental uncertainties that meant I was unable to form an opinion on the financial statements. In the circumstances we are unable to form an audit opinion.			

109 During the audit of Wand Ltd, the audit senior discovered that the depreciation methods used by the management have changed twice during the accounting period.

The management refuse to give any details of the reasoning behind the changes and the auditor has not been able to obtain sufficient evidence to support the changes. In addition, the auditor believes that the treatment could lead to a material but not pervasive misstatement.

Identify which ONE of the following opinions is appropriate in the circumstances.

Opinion	✓
Modified opinion due to an inability to obtain sufficient appropriate evidence	
Unmodified opinion	
Modified opinion due to a material misstatement	

110 Identify whether the audit opinion in the following circumstances would be modified or unmodified.

Circumstance	Opinion
Ash Ltd capitalised costs of £150,000 in respect of repairs and maintenance and included these costs in non-current assets. The amount capitalised represents 30% of Ash Ltd's profit before tax. The directors refuse to make any adjustments in respect of this matter.	PICKLIST
There is a significant uncertainty about Medlar Ltd's ability to continue as a going concern. The directors of Medlar Ltd have prepared the financial statements on a going concern basis and have fully disclosed the uncertainty in the notes to the financial statements.	PICKLIST
There is a claim against Santa Ltd which is waiting to go to court. The opinion of the Directors is that they are unlikely to have to pay any damages. The auditor agrees with this judgement. The Directors have made a full disclosure of this situation in the accounts. Although potentially material, the damages would not have a significant impact on the company.	PICKLIST
Elves Ltd has a receivable which owes the company £125,000. No payments have been made on this debt for 6 months. This represents 20% of the overall receivables figure, 2% of revenue and 15% of profit for the year. The client refuses to provide for this amount as they believe that once the new management team at the client are settled in, regular payments will start to be made.	PICKLIST

Options
Modified
Unmodified

111 The auditor's report for Alba Ltd, a large cosmetics company, is being finalised for the year ended 20X1. The directors of Alba Ltd have produced a cash flow forecast which shows a significantly worsening position over the coming 12 months. The auditors have been informed that Alba's bankers will not make a decision on the renewal of the overdraft facility until after the auditor's report is completed. The directors have agreed to include some going concern disclosures. The auditor believes the disclosures made by the directors are adequate.

Identify which ONE of the following options will be the impact on the auditor's report on the financial statements.

Statement	✓
Adverse opinion	
Unmodified opinion with a Material Uncertainty Related to Going Concern section included in the audit report	
Unmodified opinion with an Emphasis of Matter paragraph	

112 The auditor's report for Luxury Leathers Ltd, a small company selling hand-crafted leather goods, is being finalised for the year ended 20X1. The directors have prepared the accounts on the going concern basis but the auditor now believes the basis of preparation of the financial statements is incorrect.

Identify which ONE of the following options will be the impact on the auditor's report on the financial statements.

Statement	✓
Adverse opinion	
Unmodified opinion with a Material Uncertainty Related to Going Concern section included in the audit report	
Unmodified opinion with an Emphasis of Matter paragraph	

113 The audit report for See Saw Ltd, a large company which has been manufacturing, selling and installing children's play equipment to the commercial sector for over ten years, is being finalised for the year ended 20X1. Your audit manager is preparing an interim report for the audit committee and has asked you to identify if there are any issues arising which will impact upon providing an unmodified audit opinion.

Your review of the audit files identified that at the year end, See Saw Ltd received notification from one of its customers, a local privately-owned leisure centre, that a safety inspection identified equipment recently supplied does not meet new fire regulations and so must be removed and replaced. The customer had lost significant revenue as they had been unable to let children use the area housing the affected play equipment and they had informed See Saw Ltd that they intend to take legal action against them for loss of earnings. The issue with this supplier was subsequently resolved.

See Saw Ltd investigated the problem further after the year end and discovered that other work in progress is similarly affected and that inventory for those items should be written down. A note from the Finance Director stated that as this misstatement was identified after the year-end, it can be included in the financial statements for the year ended 20X2 and has refused to include any disclosure in the current year statements.

The audit manager has asked you to:

(i) explain the issues identified.

(ii) identify the audit opinion arising.

114 You are an Accounting Technician assisting in the audit of Scorpio Ltd. The financial statements of Scorpio Ltd include an investment in Taurus Ltd stated at £7.9m. Your audit team has concluded that the investment in Taurus Ltd should be recognised at £2m. The directors of Scorpio have refused to recognise the reduction in the value of the investment. The profit before tax of Scorpio Ltd is £46.7m and gross assets are £824m.

The audit manager has asked you to:

(i) explain the issues identified.

(ii) identify the audit opinion arising.

115 During the external audit of Luella Ltd for the year ended 31 December 20X2, your audit firm were unable to rely on the system of internal controls over cash sales. There were no alternative audit procedures that your firm could perform to satisfy itself that cash sales were free from material misstatement. Cash sales represent 11% of total revenue.

The audit manager has asked you to:

(i) explain the issues identified.

(ii) identify the implications for the auditor's report.

Section 2

ANSWERS TO PRACTICE QUESTIONS

PRINCIPLES AND RESPONSIBILITIES

1

Gap 1	✓
absolute	
reasonable	✓

Gap 2	✓
material	✓
all	

Gap 3	✓
express an opinion	✓
provide a guarantee	

Gap 4	✓
International Standards on Auditing	
an applicable financial reporting framework	✓

2

Statement	True ✓	False ✓
Auditors aim to give absolute assurance over the accuracy of the financial statements.		✓
A statutory audit gives reasonable assurance that the financial statements give a true and fair view.	✓	

3

Level of assurance	✓
Reasonable assurance	✓
Limited assurance	

4

Statement	True ✓	False ✓
The auditor must maintain professional scepticism throughout the duration of the audit.	✓	
The client must maintain their professional scepticism throughout the duration of the audit.		✓

KAPLAN PUBLISHING

5

Statement	True ✓	False ✓
Professional scepticism refers to the auditor not believing anything the client says to them.		✓
Professional scepticism refers to the questioning mind the auditor should maintain.	✓	

6

Gap 1	✓
directors	✓
internal auditor	

Gap 2	✓
company accountant	
external auditors	✓

Gap 3	✓
finance director	
shareholders	✓

Gap 4	✓
correct set of accounts	
true and fair view	✓

7

Gap 1	✓
experience	
independence	✓

Gap 2	✓
express an opinion	✓
provide a guarantee	

Gap 3	✓
reputation	
objectivity	✓

8

Statement	True ✓	False ✓
The auditors are responsible for preparing the financial statements on which they report.		✓
The amounts in the financial statements are stated precisely.		✓
The external auditor provides reasonable assurance on the future viability of the audited entity.		✓

ANSWERS TO PRACTICE QUESTIONS: **SECTION 2**

9

Statement	True ✓	False ✓
The IAASB works to improve the uniformity of auditing practices exclusively in the UK.		✓
The IAASB's standards contain basic principles and essential procedures together with related guidance in the form of explanatory and other material, including appendices.	✓	

10

Statement	✓
The IAASB is responsible for setting auditing standards which are compulsory throughout the world.	
The IAASB is responsible for monitoring auditors to ensure that they comply with auditing standards.	
The IAASB is responsible for investigating and disciplining auditors who fail to comply with auditing standards.	
The IAASB is responsible for setting auditing standards which facilitate the convergence of national and international auditing standards.	✓

11

Statement	✓
ISAs are best practice and can be followed by the auditor if they wish.	
ISAs are standards that compete with local standards and the auditor can choose which to use.	
ISAs are mandatory on all audits undertaken in the countries which have adopted ISAs unless the auditor has good reason for non-compliance.	✓
ISAs must be followed at all times and take precedence over Company Law of an individual country.	

12

Statement	True ✓	False ✓
The primary duty of an auditor as set out in the Companies Act 2006 requires the auditor to report to the company's members on every set of accounts requiring statutory audit.	✓	
The external auditor has a statutory duty to detect fraud as part of the main duties of the audit.		✓

AAT: AUDIT AND ASSURANCE

13

Statement	True ✓	False ✓
The external auditor has a common law duty of care towards certain third parties under the law of tort.	✓	
The external auditor has a duty to exercise 'reasonable skill and care' to the client and any breach may lead to a claim of negligence by the client.	✓	

14

Statement	True ✓	False ✓
Professional Indemnity Insurance is compulsory for all members of the Institute who have a practising certificate and are engaged in public practice, regardless of the amount of practice income.	✓	
The external auditor has a duty to ensure quality management procedures are in place within the audit practice and are implemented by their personnel.	✓	

15

Gap 1	✓
Professional competence and due care	
Professional behaviour	✓

Gap 2	✓
Independence	✓
Objectivity	

16

Situation	✓
Accepting a significant gift from an audit client.	
Owning shares in the client company.	
Acting as engagement partner of a listed audit client for more than 5 years.	✓

17

Action	✓
The matter should be reported to the tax authorities after discussion with Morris.	
The matter should be reported to the tax authorities without discussion with Morris.	
The matter should be reported to your firm's money laundering reporting officer after discussion with Morris.	
The matter should be reported to your firm's money laundering reporting officer without discussion with Morris.	✓

ANSWERS TO PRACTICE QUESTIONS: SECTION 2

18

Action	✓
The matter should be reported to the CEO of Cayman Ltd immediately.	
The matter should be reported to the CEO of Cayman Ltd after discussions with the audit manager.	
The matter should be reported to the firm's money laundering officer after discussion with the CEO.	
The matter should be reported to the firm's money laundering officer without discussion with the CEO.	✓

19

Situation	Self-interest ✓	Self-review ✓	Familiarity ✓
Performance of internal and external audits of the same client.		✓	
Overdue fees are outstanding from the client.	✓		
The audit engagement partner and the Finance Director of the client are close friends.			✓

20

Statement	True ✓	False ✓
When providing both internal and external audit services to a client, the assurance firm should use the same personnel for each of the assignments.		✓
The rotation of audit staff is an appropriate safeguard to mitigate a familiarity threat because the audit team has been in place for a number of years.	✓	

21

Statement	True ✓	False ✓
Declining an opportunity to prepare a listed company's financial statements as well as doing the audit is an appropriate safeguard to the self-review threat.	✓	
The rotation of audit staff is an appropriate safeguard to mitigate an advocacy threat when the auditor is representing the audit client in court.		✓

KAPLAN PUBLISHING

22

Gap 1	✓
Self-interest	
Intimidation	✓
Advocacy	
Self-review	

Option 1	✓
Do nothing	
Stop all audit work until payment is made	
Dismiss the partner	
Commence debt recovery process	✓

Gap 2	✓
Self-interest	✓
Intimidation	
Advocacy	
Familiarity	

Option 2	✓
Do nothing	✓
Resign from the audit	
As the fee was due to exceptional circumstances and will not reoccur do nothing	
Review whether independence is still met	

Gap 3	✓
Self-interest	
Self-review	
Advocacy	
Familiarity	✓

Option 3	✓
Do nothing	
Resign from the audit	
Rotate the partner from the audit	✓
Report the ethical threat to the audit committee	

Gap 4	✓
Self-interest	
Self-review	✓
Advocacy	
Intimidation	

Option 4	✓
Do nothing	
Remove the audit senior from the audit entirely	✓
Ensure audit senior does not work on areas she has prepared	
Report the ethical threat to the audit committee	

23

Circumstance	Requires the client's permission ✓	Does not require the client's permission ✓
The external auditor suspects that the client is involved in money laundering.		✓
The provision of evidence to support the external auditor in court.		✓
The provision of information as requested by the client's bank.	✓	

ANSWERS TO PRACTICE QUESTIONS: SECTION 2

24

Circumstance	Requires the client's permission ✓	Does not require the client's permission ✓
A request to access the previous auditor's working papers in relation to a new client.	✓	
The external auditor suspects that the client is involved in tax evasion.		✓
The external auditor suspects that a junior member of staff is involved in money laundering.		✓

25

Action	✓
Report the audit junior to the client.	
Advise the audit junior they must keep all information about the client private.	✓
Invite the friend to join your audit firm.	
Ensure full training is given to your audit junior on client confidentiality and security of sensitive information.	✓
Make a formal complaint to the rival firm about the junior's friend.	

26

Action	✓
Report the audit junior to the client.	✓
Advise the audit junior that no-one must be told about this.	
Ask the audit junior to disclose the fees being charged by their competitors.	
Ensure full training is given to your audit junior on client confidentiality and security of sensitive information.	✓

27

Statement	✓
The Code is a set of statutory provisions.	
The Code, if broken, can give rise to civil liabilities.	
Should the Code be breached a fine will be imposed.	
The Code gives rise to disclosure requirements.	✓

The UK Corporate Governance Code is not a legal requirement. The London Stock Exchange requires all listed companies to include in their annual reports a statement of compliance or non-compliance with the Code; in other words a disclosure requirement.

28

Statement	True ✓	False ✓
Corporate governance places reliance on the external auditor to ensure the company is run in the best interests of the shareholders.		✓
Corporate governance refers to how a company is directed and controlled.	✓	
Good corporate governance practises may enhance the reputation of the company.	✓	

Corporate governance places the onus on the directors to run the company in the best interests of the shareholders.

29

Statement	True ✓	False ✓
Internal auditors can never be independent of those on which they are reporting, because they are employees of the company.		✓
The UK Corporate Governance Code requires all listed companies in the UK to have an internal audit function, unless the board explain to the shareholders why this decision has been made.	✓	

30

Role	Carry out ✓	Should not carry out ✓
Monitoring the company's overall risk strategy.	✓	
Testing internal controls in the purchasing department.	✓	
Designing a system of internal control in the production department.		✓

31

Statement	True ✓	False ✓
Internal auditors should not co-operate with external auditors.		✓
Statutory audits are carried out by external auditors only.	✓	
The internal audit function forms part of the overall system of internal control.	✓	

ANSWERS TO PRACTICE QUESTIONS: SECTION 2

32

Statement	Internal auditor ✓	External auditor ✓
They provide an opinion on the financial statements.		✓
Their work is focussed on the operations of the entire business.	✓	
The role can be carried out by employees of the entity.	✓	
They are appointed by the shareholders of an entity.		✓

33

Assignment	✓
A value for money audit	✓
A management audit	
A financial audit	

34

Findings	Action
The general manager of Snow Time Ltd manned a booth during a period of staff illness and during this time a batch of tickets went missing.	Refer to audit manager
A member of staff in one of the booths has been selling tickets for the following day at a discount of 20%.	Do nothing

SYSTEMS AND CONTROLS

35

Gap 1	✓		Gap 2	✓
Segregation of duties	✓		Collusion	
Risk assessment process			Control environment	✓

Gap 3	✓
Internal audit	✓
Control environment	

36

Gap 1	✓		Gap 2	✓
Segregation of duties			Collusion	✓
Risk assessment process	✓		Control environment	

KAPLAN PUBLISHING

Gap 3	
Internal audit	
External audit	✓

37

Test	Computer assisted audit technique
Recalculation of the net book value of plant and machinery.	Audit software
Input of data with false dates to check the system identifies incorrect data for the period.	Test data
Analysis of net profit by different product classifications.	Data analytics tools

38

Test	Computer assisted audit technique
To test that timesheets are not input for non-existent employees.	Test data
Re-performance of addition or ageing of transactions.	Audit software
To discover patterns, deviations and inconsistencies within the population.	Data analytics

39

Test	Computer assisted audit technique
Comparison of the cost and net realisable value of inventory items to determine the lower value.	Audit software
Input of data with false inventory code numbers to check that the system rejects such data.	Test data
Extraction of inventory balances over £5,000 in order to carry out further testing.	Audit software

40

Statement	True	False
Using test data to trace transaction from order to inclusion the payables ledger.		✓
Walk through test of invoices being input into the system.		✓
Observation of staff processing invoices.	✓	

41

Assertion		✓
Valuation		
Classification		
Completeness		✓
Occurrence		

PLANNING, CONTROLLING AND RECORDING

42

Results of analytical procedures	Understated ✓	Overstated ✓
The results of Blue Moon Ltd show that compared to the previous year trade receivables has increased by 30% and revenue has increased by 9%.		✓
The results of Blue Moon Ltd show that compared to the previous year trade payables has decreased by 15% and purchases have decreased by 10%.	✓	
The results of Proud Pooches Ltd show that compared to the previous year trade receivables has increased by 20% and revenue has increased by 5%.		✓
The results of Proud Pooches Ltd show that compared to the previous year trade payables has decreased by 10% and purchases have decreased by 7%.	✓	

43

Options	✓
appropriate	
inappropriate	✓
acceptable	
unacceptable	

44

Component	Yes	No
Inherent risk	✓	
Control risk	✓	
Identity risk		✓
Detection risk	✓	

45

Statement	Component part
The risk that the audit procedures do not detect material misstatement in the financial statements.	Detection risk
The risk that a client's internal controls have not detected a material misstatement.	Control risk
The risk of the auditor issuing an incorrect audit opinion.	Audit risk
The risk of there being a material misstatement in the financial statements due to the nature of the client.	Inherent risk

46

Action	Increase ✓	Decrease ✓
Sales invoices are only raised for goods that have been dispatched.		✓
No initial credit checks are made on new customers to gauge their creditworthiness.	✓	
All customer receipts are correctly recorded.		✓

47

Action	Increase ✓	Decrease ✓
Due to cost saving measures, there is less segregation of duties amongst the payroll staff.		✓
The entity has recently introduced a new cash handling procedure with complete procedure notes distributed to all staff.	✓	
Management regularly review budgets and compare to forecasts to analyse the company's performance.	✓	

48

Statement	True ✓	False ✓
External auditors are able to control inherent risk and control risk so as to reduce audit risk to an acceptably low level.		✓
External auditors are able to control detection risk so as to reduce audit risk to an acceptably low level.	✓	

ANSWERS TO PRACTICE QUESTIONS: SECTION 2

49

Factor	Increase ✓	Decrease ✓	No effect ✓
The entity is committed to employing personnel with appropriate accounting and financial reporting skills.		✓	
The entity is to be sold and the purchase consideration will be determined as a multiple of reported profit.	✓		
The entity's management does not intend to remedy deficiencies in internal controls identified by the external auditor.	✓		

50

Statement	True ✓
As part of the audit planning, the auditor will determine the maximum amount of errors the auditor is willing to accept and still be satisfied that the financial statements show a true and fair view.	✓
Materiality is equally important to the auditor when expressing an opinion and the management when reviewing the financial statements.	
A material error in the financial statements may be described as the relative significance or importance of a particular matter in the context of the financial statements.	✓
A material error in the financial statements may be described as a lack of robust written processes and procedures in place to record each stage of a transaction.	

51

Statement	True ✓
Materiality is not capable of general mathematical definition as it has both qualitative and quantitative aspects.	✓
The auditor will consider a relatively small error in a month end procedure an indication of a potential material misstatement if that error is repeated each month.	✓
When determining materiality, the auditor just looks at the size of an item in comparison to the profit of the client.	
Auditing standards specify what percentage of profit would make an item material.	

52

Statement	True ✓	False ✓
Performance materiality is set a level above materiality as it only relates to the financial statements as a whole.		✓
The idea behind performance materiality is to reduce to an acceptably low level the probability that the aggregate uncorrected and undetected misstatements exceed materiality for the financial statements as a whole.	✓	
Once established, performance materiality must not be changed as the audit progresses.		✓

53

Statement	True ✓	False ✓
Performance materiality should be set at a level below the level of materiality for the financial statements as a whole.	✓	
Performance materiality is always a given percentage of overall materiality.		✓
All errors found, in excess of performance materiality, must be amended by the client in order to avoid the audit report being qualified.		✓

54

Materiality level	✓
£1.5 million	✓
£1.0 million	
£750,000	
£475,000	

Materiality ranges using traditional benchmarks:

Revenue (½% – 1%)   £620,000 – £1,240,000

Profit before tax (5% – 10%)   £475,000 – £950,000

As Nectar Ltd is a new audit client it is likely that materiality will be set at the lower end of the materiality scale to reflect the increased detection risk. Option 1 is 16% of profit and 1.2% of revenue and is therefore too high based on the traditional benchmark calculations. Options 2, 3 and 4 all sit within the ranges calculated above.

55

Gross profit margin	Payables payment period	Receivables collection period	✓
Website sales may not be accurately recorded	Payables may not be accurately recorded	Extended credit terms may have been given to customers	
Revenue may have been recognised too early	Suppliers may be withdrawing credit terms	Receivables may not be completely recorded	
Revenue may not have occurred	Purchase invoices may have been recorded twice	Receivables may not exist	
Website sales may not be completely recorded	Payables may not be completely recorded	Receivables may be overvalued	✓

Gross profit margin

The ratio has decreased from 26% to 17% which indicates that website sales may not be completely recorded.

If sales had not occurred, the revenue balance would be overstated and the gross profit margin would increase.

If revenue had been recognised too early, the revenue balance would be overstated and the gross profit margin would increase.

Payables payment period

The ratio has decreased from 75 to 40 days which indicates understatement of payables i.e. payables may not be completely recorded.

Suppliers withdrawing credit terms is a business risk, not an audit risk.

If purchase invoices have been recorded twice, the payables balance would be overstated and the payables payment period would increase.

Receivables collection period

The ratio has increased from 29 to 38 days which indicates that receivables may be overvalued.

Extended credit terms may have been given to customers is not an audit risk.

If receivables are not completely recorded, the receivables balance would be understated and the receivables collection period would decrease.

56

Working paper	Reason for preparation
Independence questionnaire completed by each member of the audit team.	Compliance with independence and ethical requirements
Copies of cash flow and profit forecasts and post year-end management accounts.	Assess the going concern status
Details of the review of assets in the factory whilst attending the inventory count.	Supporting valuation of assets

AAT: AUDIT AND ASSURANCE

57

Statement	True ✓	False ✓
Working papers must only be prepared in electronic form to ensure confidentiality and security.		✓
There are two main types of file for audit working papers; the permanent audit file and the current audit file.	✓	
The date of the working papers and the name of the person preparing the file should be clearly stated on all documents.	✓	

58

Statement	True ✓	False ✓
The audit working papers are prepared and collated during the audit and should be retained in connection with the performance of the audit.	✓	
The permanent audit file should not contain any copies of statutory or legal regulations or papers.		✓
The current audit file should include schedules showing the results of audit tests carried out.	✓	

59

Statement	True ✓	False ✓
The auditor's working papers provide adequate evidence of the work that has been carried out and the conclusions reached contain sufficient appropriate audit evidence to support the conclusions made.	✓	
The auditor will rely on a designated staff member from the client's workforce to assist in the compilation of the current audit file.		✓
The permanent audit files contain information of continuing importance to the audit such as board minutes of relevance, previous years' signed accounts, analytical reviews and engagement letters.	✓	

60

Statement	True ✓	False ✓
Working papers are prepared by the external auditor because there is a legal requirement to do so.		✓
The objective of working papers is to provide evidence that the audit was planned and performed in accordance with International Standards on Auditing.	✓	
Working papers should contain the name of who performed the audit work and the date it was performed.	✓	

ANSWERS TO PRACTICE QUESTIONS: SECTION 2

61

Statement	True ✓
The detailed content of each type of audit working paper is strictly detailed in the ISAs.	
The primary objective of working papers is to prove to the audit partner that the work was done.	
Working papers should clearly state which year-end they pertain to and show evidence that they have been reviewed.	✓

62 Multiple sites

- The external auditor may not be able to visit all of the sites. They will have to establish which ones to visit, and then visit the others on a rotational basis.

Wages

- Casual workers are paid cash in hand which increases the risk of misappropriation of cash.
- PAYE/NIC may not be calculated correctly.

Cash sales

- Significant number of cash sales which increases the risk of misappropriation of cash.
- Risk of understatement of sales.
- No reconciliations of tills
    - Cash could be misappropriated.
    - Sales could be understated.
    - Lack of control from Head Office.

Purchases

- There is no check of invoices to goods actually received.
- Company may pay for goods not received or goods that were of low quality.

63 Receivables

- Customers are invoiced after installation which could cause issues collecting money.
- Risk of irrecoverable receivables.

Revenue recognition

- The revenue for the service support contracts should be spread over the period to which the contract relates. This could result in overstatement of revenue if not done correctly.
- Deferred income may be misstated on the statement of financial position.

Inventory

- Different types of inventory which could cause issues for valuation purposes.
- Valuation of WIP is notoriously difficult due to the nature and establishing the stage of completion.

KAPLAN PUBLISHING

AAT: AUDIT AND ASSURANCE

Foreign currency transactions

- Risk of inappropriate exchange rates used which can cause errors in purchases, payables and inventory.

Warranty provision

- This is a judgmental area in the financial statements.
- Will need to understand the assumptions underlying the provision.
- How accurate has the provision been in the past?

64
- Going concern risk if company fails to comply with the terms of the loan.
- Misclassification of the loan in the financial statements i.e. split between current and non-current liability.
- Manipulation of financial statements to meet loan covenants.
- Incorrect calculation of interest.
- Failure to record loan and loan repayments.
- Incorrect disclosure of the loan terms and interest.
- Project incorrectly capitalised and depreciated.

65
- Incorrect classification of the lorries within non-current assets.
- Incorrect classification of the finance agreement within liabilities i.e. split between current and non-current liability.
- Incorrect calculation of the finance liability.
- Inappropriate depreciation policy.
- Incorrect calculation of depreciation.
- Inaccurate cost figures used.
- Incorrect calculation of interest on the loan.
- Incorrect disclosure of the loan terms and interest.
- Recording purchase in wrong period.
- Failure to record the new assets at all.
- Failure to record loan repayments.

66
- Statutory fines and penalties which would need to be provided for in the financial statements.
- Provisions may be omitted or understated in the financial statements.
- Increased insurance premiums which could have an adverse effect on cash flow which could lead to going concern issues.
- Loss of reputation may lead to forced closure which could lead to going concern issues and may mean the financial statements need to be prepared on the break up basis.

67
- Director's assessment is subject to uncertainty.
- Non-current provision represents 1% (20X3) and 1% (20X2) of revenue.
- Current provision represents 1.1% (20X3) and 1.25% (20X2) of revenue.
- Inconsistent with the increase in extended warranty period from two to five years.
- Possible understatement.

Alternative calculations:

Marks will be awarded where calculations are presented as follows:

Increase in non-current provision of 14.2%

Increase in current provision of 0.1%

Total of current and non-current provision 2.1% (20X3) and 2.25% (20X2)

Increase in warranty provision of 6.9%

Increase in revenue of 14.8%

68 20X2 salary costs adjusted for:
- 3% pay rise
- 8% growth in employees

Average pay per employee compared:
- with prior year
- with budget
- by each office

Calculate expected PAYE/NI based on expected gross salaries.

Average monthly wage bill per office to identify outliers.

69
- Misstatement of payroll costs and liabilities to HMRC.
- Unrecorded interest for late payment.
- Unrecorded provision for damages/breach of contract or disclosure as contingent liability for damages.

70
- The revaluation is a subjective measurement and may not have been carried out correctly, or may have been recorded inappropriately.
- The loss on sale of plant may indicate that useful lives are not estimated reliably.
- The loss may have been calculated incorrectly, or disposed of assets may not have been correctly eliminated from the accounting records.
- The depreciation charge for the year seems inappropriately low compared to the prior year and the increased value of non-current assets, indicating a potential misstatement.
- Additions during the year may have been capitalised inappropriately, instead of being expensed.
- Errors may have occurred in relation to cut-off, and the amounts recorded.
- Useful lives of new assets may be inappropriately estimated.

71 Audit approach

- Substantive based approach
- Lack of internal controls (high control risk) due to:
  - Lack of segregation of duties; and
  - The possibility of unreliable software
- Higher detection risk associated with new audit
- Greater emphasis on tests of details
- Limited use of analytical procedures as there are no prior year comparatives and a lack of cumulative auditor knowledge.

AUDIT TECHNIQUES

72

Procedure	Test of control ✓	Test of detail ✓	Analytical procedure ✓
Developing an expectation of payroll costs by taking into account last year's payroll figure, annual pay rises and starters and leavers.			✓
Reviewing purchase orders to see if they have been approved by a relevant member of staff.	✓		
Recalculating PAYE and NIC costs for payroll.		✓	
Calculating receivables and payables days and comparing to the prior year.			✓
Reviewing bank reconciliations to ensure they have been prepared and reviewed by an appropriate person.	✓		

73

Information	Accuracy ✓	Classification ✓	Existence ✓
Receivables circularisation letter			✓
After date receipts			✓
Description of goods		✓	

74

Information	Valuation ✓	Completeness ✓	Existence ✓
The auditor seeks assurance that the asset or liability is recorded at the correct value.	✓		
A full inventory check is performed with the auditor verifying inventory sheets to inventory on shelves.			✓

75

Information	Component part
Date of the invoice	Cut-off
Description of the item purchased	Classification
Monetary amount	Accuracy
Addressee of the invoice	Rights and obligations

76

Gap 1	✓
Block sampling	✓
Stratification	

Gap 2	✓
Haphazard sampling	
Systematic sampling	✓

Gap 3	✓
Sampling risk	
Non-sampling risk	✓

77

Factor	Increase ✓	Decrease ✓	No effect ✓
Being able to test very easily 90% of the sales invoices by way of a proof in total.		✓	
Internal controls are found to be weak and not operating effectively.	✓		
The audit client requesting that the auditor reduces the amount of testing.			✓

78

Circumstance	Tests of controls and substantive procedures	Substantive procedures only, with no tests of controls
The audited entity was only set up a year ago, and there is only one member of staff in the accounting department.		✓
There is no segregation of duties within the accounting department of the client.		✓
The client has an internal audit department which reviews controls throughout the year.	✓	

79

Circumstance	Tests of controls and substantive procedures	Substantive procedures only, with no tests of controls
The entity has a strong control environment.	✓	
A large fraud has been identified which came about due to the collusion of several members of staff.		✓
A new accounting package was introduced at the beginning of the year and there have been significant operational deficiencies with the new system.		✓

80

Procedure	Test of control	Substantive procedure
Perform tests on the supplier statement reconciliation process to confirm the completeness of payables.		✓
Reviewing credit control procedures for recoverability of receivables.	✓	

ANSWERS TO PRACTICE QUESTIONS: SECTION 2

81

Procedure	Test of control	Substantive procedure
Comparison of the current year's revenue figure with the previous year's figure.		✓
Observation of the despatch procedures in respect of goods leaving an entity's warehouse.	✓	
Vouching of an addition to non-current assets to the supplier's invoice.		✓

82

No further action	Refer to supervisor
✓	✓
	✓

83

No further action	Refer to supervisor
✓	✓
	✓

84

No further action	Refer to supervisor
✓	✓
	✓

85

No further action	Refer to supervisor
✓	✓
✓	

86

No further action	Refer to supervisor
✓	✓
✓	

87

No further action	Refer to supervisor
✓	✓
	✓

88

No further action	Refer to supervisor
✓	✓
✓	

89

No further action	Refer to supervisor
✓	✓
✓	

90
- Obtain a breakdown of the work in progress balance, cast it and ensure the total agrees to the figure in the financial statements.
- Test a sample of entries for materials to purchase invoices.
- Complete weekly reconciliations of cash sales to receivables.
- Trace a sample of invoices to costing records.
- Trace a sample of timesheet/payroll details to the costing records.
- Carry out analytical procedures to determine overall performance.
- Discuss with management process for determining stage of completion and determine if reasonable.
- If applicable, discuss the method of calculating the overhead absorption rate and re-calculate to ensure reasonable.

91
- Obtain a breakdown of non-current assets, cast it and ensure the total agrees to the figure in the financial statements.
- Select a sample of items from the asset register and then physically inspect them to confirm existence.
- Select a sample of visible assets and inspect the relevant entry in the asset register to confirm the latter is complete.
- Select a sample of items from the register and inspect their source ownership documents (such as invoices, lease agreements) to confirm the terms of acquisition and, hence, ownership.
- Add up all items in the asset register to confirm the documents' mathematical accuracy.
- Recalculate a sample of depreciation charges to confirm the mathematical accuracy of the register.
- Compare the totals on the register with that of the nominal ledger to confirm the accuracy of financial records/ledgers.
- Review statement of profit or loss accounts such as repairs and renewals to ensure all assets have been capitalised.

92
- Obtain a breakdown of receivables, cast it and ensure the total agrees to the figure in the financial statements.
- Stratify the population in order to conduct sample testing.
- Perform a direct confirmation of a sample of receivables.
- Obtain aged receivables analysis and cast for accuracy.
- Review reconciliation from receivables ledger control account to receivables ledger.
- Perform after date cash test on a sample of receivables.
- Calculate receivables days and compare with prior year.
- Compare ageing of receivables with prior year.
- Review aged receivables list for any overdue debts and discuss with Credit Controller.
- Review above debts for inclusion in specific bad debt provision.
- Enquire as to methodology behind any general bad debt provision.
- Recalculate general bad debt provision based on client's methodology.
- Agree receivables figure to draft financial statements.
- Agree ageing of a sample of specific receivables by agreeing to invoices.
- Review receivables ledger for any credit balances.

93 (i) There are a number of weaknesses in the control activities at Funfit Gyms.

Weakness include:

- the reception staff are in a position to be able to sell towels, water bottles and sports equipment for cash and not record the details on the spreadsheet. This means that cash could be misappropriated by the reception staff.

- the reception staff have full access to the product inventory. This means that may be misappropriated by reception staff.

- the key to the cash box is lying on display on top of the reception desk so may be at risk of being taken by others. There is no detail to suggest the area has restricted access. This means that the cash box could be opened by unauthorised persons.

- there is no limit on the amount of cash held in the cash box. This provides opportunity for theft of a substantial amount of cash, particularly at weekends when the box is not taken to the accountant's office to be emptied.

- the recording of products sold and day bookings relies on the reception staff entering accurate details on a timely basis. There is no suggestion that reconciliations are undertaken between the spreadsheet and inventory or the spreadsheet and number of individuals using the gym.

During busy periods, stress may be placed on reception staff who may find it difficult to provide appropriate levels of service at the same time as recording necessary information and keeping cash safe.

AAT: AUDIT AND ASSURANCE

Given the number of weaknesses in the control system, particularly preventative and detective controls, reliance cannot be placed on the control systems at Funfit Gyms. As a result, full substantive testing should be undertaken. In addition, given the opportunity for irregularities as identified above, emphasis should be placed on substantive procedures designed to ensure that possible errors could be detected.

The substantive procedures are likely to include a focus on analytical review to identify any differences in sales/monies banked at particular times and these could also be analysed against staff shift patterns. Such an analysis may highlight patterns and inconsistencies which can then be analysed by more detailed testing.

(ii) Controls identified should be linked the discussion in part (i) and may include the following:

- Key to inventory store held in a secure location by the manager i.e. not available to reception staff
- Regular inventory checks and reconciliations of gym products by staff other than those on reception
- Spreadsheet reconciled to day bookings and gym products on a regular basis
- Limited access to cash box i.e. key not left on display
- Limits maintained of amounts held in cash box
- CCTV of reception
- Implement a token/receipt system so that all day customers have to show proof of payment when they enter the main gym area.

94 (i) Tests of control:

To ensure adequacy of controls of system of accounting for completeness of revenue.

For a sample of days, check that parking tickets have been signed as evidence of the fee charged having been checked by head office personnel. The cash banked per the statement should be agreed to the summary of fees taken.

For a sample of parking tickets, check that the issue from, and subsequent return to, head office was controlled, and that any missing tickets were fully investigated.

(ii) A **test of control** is an audit procedure to test the effectiveness of an internal control used by a client to prevent or detect material misstatements in their financial statements. Depending on the results of this test, auditors may choose to rely upon a client's system of internal control as part of their auditing activities.

95 (i) **Membership fees**

- Compare the list of members as at 1 October 2020 to 1 October 2021 to determine how many members did not renew their membership during the year. This is normally approximately 10%.
- Confirm total membership fees are correct by performing analytical procedures. Membership revenue should be:

430 members less 10% = 387, 387 × £400 = £154,800, 50 new members at 50% fee = 50 × £200 = £10,000, Total fee income £164,800.

- Agree the membership fee revenue to the financial statements. If the amount is materially different enquire of the treasurer why this is the case.

(ii) Audit tests on expenditure

- Perform analytical procedures on expenditure this year compared to last year. Obtain reasons for any unusual amounts, e.g. increased expenditure on tennis balls due to increased number of matches.

- For a sample of purchase invoices, ensure recorded in the cash records and that the amount and analysis of expenditure (e.g. lighting, tennis balls, etc) is correct.

- Obtain the statements from the debit card used by the club official – trace items from the statements to the cash records to ensure all expenditure has been recorded.

- For a sample of entries in the cash records, agree to the bank statements to ensure they represent actual expenditure.

- Cast the cash records to ensure they are arithmetically correct.

- For totals in the cash records, agree to the trial balance and financial statements, ensuring that the presentation in the accounts is correct (e.g. stated as tennis balls, line painting, etc).

96 (i)

Test Data	Reason for test
Input of an order for a negative number of tennis racquets	Ensures that only positive quantities are accepted – although the company cannot despatch negative quantities anyway.
Input of an order for ten tennis racquets	There are reasonableness checks in the system to identify possible input errors. A warning message should appear on screen asking the customer to confirm any order for more than say two racquets.
Input of an order without payment details	Ensures that orders are paid for prior to despatch – being completed this also limits the number of bad debts.
Input of invalid inventory code	Ensures that the computer detects the invalid code and presents an error message rather than taking the nearest code and accepting that.
Input of invalid customer credit card details	Online checking of credit card details to the credit card company ensures that goods cannot be despatched without payment. This will also limit the number of bad debts.
Input of invalid address	Ensures that the address and post code are valid, possibly by accessing a database of valid codes. If the code is not valid an error message should be displayed. This ensures that goods are only despatched to valid addresses.

(ii) Difficulties of using audit software

- Substantial set up costs because the client's procedures and files must be understood in detail before the audit software can be used to access and interrogate those files.

- Audit software may not be available for the specific systems set up by the client, especially if those systems are bespoke. The cost of writing audit software to test those systems may be difficult to justify against the possible benefits on the audit.

- The software may produce too much output either due to poor design of the software or using inappropriate parameters on a test. The auditor may waste considerable time checking what appear to be transactions with errors in them when the fault is actually in the audit software.

- Checking the client's files in a live situation. There is the danger that the client's systems are disrupted by the audit program. The data files can be used offline, but this will mean ensuring that the files are true copies of the live files.

(iii) Audit tests

Audit software	Reason for test
Calculation check of the revenue records	Ensures that the computerised revenue records have been cast correctly and helps to verify the revenue balance in the financial statements.
Analysis of the aging of inventory items	Help to detect inventory items which are relatively old which may need valuing at net realisable value rather than cost.
Selecting a sample of inventory at the end of the year as part of the physical verification	Removes bias from sample selection as well as being quicker than selecting the items manually.
Selecting a sample of sales invoices for checking to despatch documentation	Removes bias from sample selection as well as being quicker than selecting the items manually.
Checking completeness of sales invoice numbers	Ensures that all sales invoices are recorded.
Check that all sales invoices have been paid for	All sales are paid for on ordering, unpaid sales would be a violation of systems rules and would need to be investigated by the auditor.
List large credit notes (perhaps more than five racquets) for investigation by the auditor	The auditor will find reasons for the return – this is also a check on the accuracy of the ordering system – ordering errors may result in customers returning goods later.

ANSWERS TO PRACTICE QUESTIONS: SECTION 2

97 (a) Deficiencies in counting inventory

Deficiency	Reason for deficiency	How to overcome weakness:
Inventory sheets stated the quantity of items expected to be found in the store	Count teams will focus on finding that number of items making undercounting of inventory more likely – teams stop counting when 'correct' number of items found.	Count sheets should not state the quantity of items so as not to pre-judge how many units will be found.
Count staff were all drawn from the stores	Count staff are also responsible for the inventory. There could be a temptation to hide errors or missing inventory that they have removed from the store illegally.	Count teams should include staff who are not responsible for inventory to provide independence in the count.
Count teams allowed to decide which areas to count	There is a danger that teams will either omit inventory from the count or even count inventory twice due to lack of precise instructions on where to count.	Each team should be given a precise area of the store to count.
Count sheets were not signed by the staff carrying out the count	Lack of signature makes it difficult to raise queries regarding items counted because the actual staff carrying out the count are not known.	All count sheets should be signed to confirm who actually carried out the count of individual items.
Inventory not marked to indicate it has been counted	As above, there is a danger that inventory will be either omitted or included twice in the count.	Inventory should be marked in some way to show that it has been counted to avoid this error.
Recording information on the count sheets in pencil	Recording in pencil means that the count sheets could be amended after the count has taken place, not just during the count. The inventory balances will then be incorrectly recorded.	Count sheets should be completed in ink.
Count sheets for inventory not on the pre-numbered count sheets were only numbered when used	It is possible that the additional inventory sheets could be lost as there is no overall control of the sheets actually being used. Sheets may not be numbered by the teams, again giving rise to the possibility of loss.	All inventory sheets, including those for 'extra' inventory, should be pre-numbered.

KAPLAN PUBLISHING

71

(b) **(i)** The aim of a test of control is to check that an audit client's system of internal control is operating effectively.

The aim of a substantive procedure is to ensure that there are no material errors at the assertion level in the client's financial statements.

(ii) Regarding the inventory count:

Test of control

Observe the count teams ensuring that they are counting in accordance with the client's inventory count instructions.

Substantive procedure

Record the condition of items of inventory to ensure that the valuation of those items is correct on the final inventory summaries.

98 **(i)** Ask the sales manager for a schedule of irrecoverable debts that make up the total in the accounts. Add up the figures and agree the balance to the irrecoverable debts total in the financial statements.

(ii) Inspect all customer files and correspondence relating to each customer deemed an irrecoverable debt to ensure that sufficient effort has been made by Green Co to recover the debt. This may include inspecting solicitor's letters and debt collection agency correspondence.

(iii) Inspect the aged debt's analysis to identify any debts still outstanding e.g. more than 60 days old. Ask the sales manager why the old debts are still outstanding and what action is Green Co taking to recover the debts. Consider if the trade receivables allowance is sufficient in light of the old debts identified.

(iv) Ask the sales manager how the allowance for receivables was calculated for inclusion in the financial statements e.g. specific overdue or disputed invoices identified. Recalculate the allowance and confirm the figure in the financial statements is correct.

(v) Review the results of the circularisation of receivables to determine whether they indicate that a write-off or allowance may be required.

(vi) Review cash received after the accounting year end to determine whether any debts that may be considered bad have actually been recovered.

99 **(i)** Obtain from the client a schedule of movements in non-current assets for the year, check the additions on the schedule, agree the totals to the amounts in the draft accounts and the closing balances to the nominal ledger.

(ii) Recalculate the opening balances on the schedule and in the draft accounts to:

- the closing balances in the preceding years accounts; and
- closing balances in the underlying books and records for the preceding period.

(iii) Vouch additions to the non-current assets to purchase invoices or lease agreements, and the entry in the nominal ledger. Also, check that the item has been included in the non-current asset register.

Compare disposals to supporting documentation (e.g. sales invoice) and consider whether the disposal proceeds are reasonable. Check the cost and accumulated depreciation at the date of disposal to the non-current asset register and check that this has been properly deducted on the schedule (in (i) above) and in the nominal ledger. Check that the profit or loss on disposal of the asset has been correctly treated in the nominal ledger.

ANSWERS TO PRACTICE QUESTIONS: SECTION 2

(iv) Recalculate the additions of cost, accumulated depreciation and depreciation expense of the individual non-current assets in the non-current asset register to the amounts on the schedule, draft accounts and nominal ledger.

(v) Physically inspect a sample of non-current assets. The check should be performed from both the non-current asset register to the non-current assets (which checks that the non-current assets in the register exist) and from the non-current asset to the non-current asset register (which checks that the non-current assets which exist are included in the non-current asset register, and hence in the accounts i.e. complete). In verifying non-current assets, it is important to check the serial number on the item (or vehicle registration number). However, this is not possible for most fixtures and fittings, so only agreement of the description is possible.

If some of the vehicles are located in other parts of the country, obtain a certificate of existence signed by the user of the vehicle (e.g. for salesperson's cars).

(vi) Enquire as to whether the depreciation rates are reasonable. If there are losses on sale of non-current assets, it is an indication that depreciation rates are inadequate. If there are profits on the sale of non-current assets or a significant proportion of the non-current assets are fully written off, then it is an indication that depreciation rates are too high. However, auditors are more likely to accept too high a depreciation rate than too low a depreciation rate, as they would argue this is a prudent approach.

Non-current assets may become obsolete (e.g. a depreciation rate of 10% on cost would be unrealistic for portable computers).

The auditor would consider whether the remaining lives of the existing non-current assets are realistic by asking the company's senior management and looking at the condition of the non-current assets.

(vii) Consider whether there are any obsolete or unused non-current assets, by asking management, inspecting the minutes of board and management meetings and looking at the non-current assets in the factory. Obsolete non-current assets should be written down to estimated disposal value, and the auditor would consider whether unused non-current assets will be used again – if they are unlikely to be used again, they should be treated in the same way as obsolete non-current assets. By the term 'obsolete' the auditor would mean assets which are of no more economic value to the company – a computer may be technically obsolete, but if it is still used for processing accounting data (or other tasks), it is not 'obsolete' in terms of the discussion above.

(viii) Inspect vehicle registration documents for motor vehicles. Check them to the non-current assets register. The vehicle registration document is not a document of title, but it is good evidence of the existence of the vehicle and that the company may own it.

(ix) Inspect the deeds of the property – the latest conveyance should be in the name of the company. Also the auditor could check with the land registry that the land is registered in the company's name.

100 (i) Agree reported trade payables values to trade payables control account reconciliation and underlying working papers/schedules.

(ii) Carry out analytical procedures and make enquiries as appropriate, ensuring that 54% increase on previous year balance makes sense taking all matters into account.

(iii) Review reconciliation of supplier account statements to trade payable ledger balances, prepared by Pear Co staff. Enquire into any abnormalities and carry out further reconciliations as required.

(iv) Review cut-off procedures for goods received and recognition of amounts payable at 30 April 20X5. Test to ensure accuracy.

(v) Review unmatched goods received notes (goods received but associated invoice not received at 30 April 20X5), and ensure inclusion in trade payables value.

(vi) Review trade payables control account postings immediately, prior to and post 30 April 20X5 and enquire into veracity of unusual items.

(vii) Use CAATs as appropriate to identify for further investigation, long outstanding balances including those with no recent activity and accounts containing unusual debit entries.

101 (i) Inspect relevant correspondence (including legal correspondence) relating to the damages claim and compare the value of the claim as reported in the statement of profit or loss to underlying estimates and opinions available.

(ii) Discuss the nature and amount of the claim with the responsible officials of the client, and enquire as to underlying rationale of the sum provided. If appropriate, with client permission, seek confirmation of the value of claim from an independent expert.

(iii) Inspect the minutes of board or management meetings to obtain substantiating evidence as to the existence and nature of the claim.

(iv) Review appropriate expense accounts to identify expenditure already incurred in connection with the claim and costs possibly duplicated in the final provision.

(v) Obtain permission from the directors of Apple Co and write to the company legal advisers to confirm the likelihood of Apple Co having to settle the claim and the likely value of the claim.

(vi) Review disclosure of the provision in the financial statements in accordance with relevant international financial reporting standards.

COMPLETION AND REPORTING

102

Uncorrected misstatement	Material	
		✓
Expenses payments to staff of £21,600 not authorised.	Yes	
	No	✓
Errors in recording returned products resulting in overstatement of sales totalling £89,923.	Yes	✓
	No	

ANSWERS TO PRACTICE QUESTIONS: SECTION 2

103

Gap 1			Gap 2	
is appropriate			The matter involves management judgement	✓
is not appropriate	✓		Other procedures can be performed which provide more reliable evidence	✓

Gap 3			Gap 4	
is appropriate	✓		The matter involves management judgement	✓
is not appropriate			Other procedures can be performed which provide more reliable evidence	

104 (i) Consequences

- Equipment recorded in the register may not exist or may have been stolen.
- Acquisitions or disposals may not be recorded.
- Equipment may be fully written down but still in use.
- Equipment may be impaired and consequently overvalued.
- Depreciation charges on the equipment may be inappropriate.

(ii) Recommendations

- Periodic reconciliation of:
    - physical equipment to register to ensure completeness of recording
    - entries in the register to physical equipment to ensure existence and in good condition.
- Reconciliation to be performed independent of custodian.
- Differences to be reported and investigated.
- Monitoring of procedures to ensure checks undertaken.

105 (i) Consequences

- Relevant price may not be the most up to date.
- Receivables ledger clerk may update the price incorrectly.
- Receivables ledger clerk may manipulate the sales price on the master file fraudulently.
- Sales invoices may be raised incorrectly due to incorrect sales price being used.

(ii) Recommendations

- Sales director should review and authorise all sales price updates.
- Sales director should inform the receivables ledger clerk of updated with written confirmation to ensure an audit trail.
- Reconciliation to be performed between a sample of sales invoices with the sales price on the master file.

KAPLAN PUBLISHING

106 (i) Consequences

- Goods may be broken/damaged on arrival and we cannot later claim from the supplier.
- We may accept goods which were not as ordered, or not ordered at all.
- The wrong person may be emailed and the goods may not be claimed.
- The person who ordered the goods may not get the email and may re-order the goods thinking they have not arrived.
- The goods could be stolen or damaged while in the warehouse waiting to be collected.

(ii) Recommendations

- A copy of the purchase order should be sent to the warehouse in preparation for the goods arriving.
- The copy order should clearly state who should be contacted when the goods arrive.
- The warehouse staff should check the quality of the goods when they arrive.
- The warehouse staff should agree the content of the goods to the details on the order.
- The warehouse staff should complete a Goods Received Note (GRN) detailing the goods received and evidencing that they have performed the above checks.
- The goods received notes should be sequentially numbered.
- A copy of the GRN should be sent to the person who placed the order to say the goods are to be collected.
- When they come to the warehouse to collect the goods, they should sign the warehouse copy of the GRN to evidence collection.
- The warehouse should keep a copy of the completed GRN with their copy of the order.

107 (i) Deficiency

The buyer is responsible for ordering goods, the custody of goods and for the authorisation of invoices when they are received.

Consequence

There is a risk of fraud and error due to the involvement of only the buyer in these areas.

Recommendation

To reduce the possibility of fraud and error, the company should ensure that there is proper segregation of duties in the ordering, purchase and custody and recording of inventory.

ANSWERS TO PRACTICE QUESTIONS: SECTION 2

(ii) Deficiency

Inventory is ordered by telephone.

Consequence

There is a risk of unauthorised/wrong goods being ordered and delivered.

Recommendation

The company should introduce a system of documentation to support the ordering process. Purchase orders should be used which are authorised by an independent responsible official of the company. Purchase orders should be pre-printed, pre-numbered and subject to rigid custody controls. The company should also draw up a list of approved suppliers – orders should be placed only with these suppliers unless specific authorisation is obtained to use other suppliers.

(iii) Deficiency

Goods received by the company are not checked for quality.

Consequence

Sub-standard goods, defective or damaged goods could be accepted and paid for by the company.

Recommendation

Competent and trained personnel should check all goods received. They should prepare signed goods received notes for each delivery.

108

Statement	Qualified opinion ✓	Unmodified opinion ✓	Disclaimer of opinion ✓
In our opinion: The financial statements give a true and fair view, in accordance with UK Generally Accepted Accounting Practice, of the state of the company's affairs as at 31 March 2008 and of its profit for the year then ended. The financial statements have been properly prepared in accordance with the Companies Act 2006; and the information given in the Directors' Report is consistent with the financial statements.		✓	
Extract: I planned my audit so as to obtain all the information and explanations which I considered necessary in order to provide me with sufficient evidence to give reasonable assurance that the financial statements are free from material misstatements. In forming my opinion I also evaluated the overall adequacy of the presentation of information in the financial statements. However, the evidence available to me was limited by the fundamental uncertainties that meant I was unable to form an opinion on the financial statements. In the circumstances we are unable to form an audit opinion.			✓

109

Opinion	✓
Modified opinion due to an inability to obtain sufficient appropriate evidence	✓
Unmodified opinion	
Modified opinion due to a material misstatement	

ANSWERS TO PRACTICE QUESTIONS: SECTION 2

110

Circumstance	Computer assisted audit technique
Ash Ltd capitalised costs of £150,000 in respect of repairs and maintenance and included these costs in non-current assets. The amount capitalised represents 30% of Ash Ltd's profit before tax. The directors refuse to make any adjustments in respect of this matter.	Modified
There is a significant uncertainty about Medlar Ltd's ability to continue as a going concern. The directors of Medlar Ltd have prepared the financial statements on a going concern basis and have fully disclosed the uncertainty in the notes to the financial statements.	Not modified
There is a claim against Santa Ltd which is waiting to go to court. The opinion of the Directors is that they are unlikely to have to pay any damages. The auditor agrees with this judgement. The Directors have made a full disclosure of this situation in the accounts. Although potentially material, the damages would not have a significant impact on the company.	Not modified
Elves Ltd has a receivable which owes the company £125,000. No payments have been made on this debt for 6 months. This represents 20% of the overall receivables figure, 2% of revenue and 15% of profit for the year. The client refuses to provide for this amount as they believe that once the new management team at the client are settled in, regular payments will start to be made.	Modified

111

Statement	✓
Adverse opinion	
Unmodified opinion with a Material Uncertainty Related to Going Concern section included in the audit report	✓
Unmodified opinion with an Emphasis of Matter paragraph	

112

Statement	✓
Adverse opinion	✓
Unmodified opinion with a Material Uncertainty Related to Going Concern section included in the audit report	
Unmodified opinion with an Emphasis of Matter paragraph	

AAT: AUDIT AND ASSURANCE

113 (i) Issues identified

- Discussions should be held with the Finance Director as to why they are refusing to make the amendment/disclosure in the current financial year.
- Assess the materiality of the inventory issue. If immaterial, the amount should be included in the schedule of unadjusted differences. If material, the matter should be assessed through further audit procedures.
- The audit opinion will depend on the materiality of the issue, which should be assessed.

(ii) Audit opinion

- If material but not pervasive, a modified audit opinion is required and the issue would represent a material misstatement. This requires a qualified opinion as well as a basis for qualified opinion paragraph.
- The opinion paragraph should use the wording 'except for' which gives details of the inventory write-off.

114 (i) Issues identified

- There is a misstatement in the value of the investment of £5.9m (impairment).
- The misstatement represents 12.3% of profit before tax and is therefore a material issue.
- The issue is not classed as pervasive because it represents 0.7% of gross assets and is not a substantial proportion/isolated to individual item in the financial statements.

(ii) Audit opinion

- A modified audit opinion is required as the issue represents a material misstatement. This requires a qualified opinion as well as a basis for qualified opinion paragraph.
- The opinion paragraph should use the wording 'except for' which gives details of the misstatement in the value of the investment.

115 (i) Issues identified

- There is an inability to obtain sufficient appropriate audit evidence over the cash sales.
- The issue is material but not pervasive as it is confined to a specific element of the financial statements and does not represent a substantial proportion of the financial statements.

(ii) Implications for the auditor's report

- A modified audit opinion is required as the issue represents a material misstatement. This requires a qualified opinion as well as a basis for qualified opinion paragraph.
- The opinion paragraph should use the wording 'except for' which gives details of the misstatement in the value of the investment.
- Report by exception under CA06: not able to obtain all information necessary and adequate accounting records not maintained.

Section 3

MOCK ASSESSMENT QUESTIONS

The assessment is 2.5 hours long and consists of 6 tasks. You should attempt all of the tasks. Each task is independent and you will not need to refer to previous tasks.

TASK 1 (10 MARKS)

This task is about the conceptual and regulatory framework, corporate governance and internal audit.

(a) Identify whether the following statements about levels of assurance are true or false.

Statement	True ✓	False ✓
Reasonable assurance is always expressed with a positive conclusion.		
Limited assurance can never be given.		

(2 marks)

(b) You are the external auditor of a company whose board have decided to disband their internal audit team, and have given you reasons for doing so.

Identify which ONE of the following statements is correct in relation to internal audit.

Statement	✓
Having an internal audit function is a requirement for UK Listed Companies under the UK Corporate Governance Code so your audit report should identify this as inappropriate.	
If the board explain to shareholders why this decision has been made, it is in line with the UK Corporate Governance Code.	

(1 mark)

(c) Identify which TWO of the following are correct in respect of the UK Corporate Governance Code.

Statement	✓
The board of directors should establish procedures to minimise risk.	
The company should elect separate people as chairperson and chief executive.	
The board of directors should establish an Audit Committee with a minimum membership of five non-executive directors.	
All UK companies are required by law to comply with the code.	

(2 marks)

(d) **Identify the correct option for each responsibility.**

Responsibility	Options
Preparation of the financial statements.	PICKLIST
Ensure auditor recommendations are actioned.	PICKLIST
Produce a report on whether the financial statements give a true and fair view.	PICKLIST

Options
External auditors
Board of directors
Audit committee
Internal auditors

(3 marks)

(e) **Complete the following statement:**

An external audit gives _____GAP 1_____ assurance that the financial statements are true and fair, which means that they are free from _____GAP 2_____ misstatement, whether due to fraud or error.

Gap 1	✓
absolute	
reasonable	
limited	

Gap 2	✓
all	
major	
material	

(2 marks)

TASK 2 (15 MARKS)

This task is about professional ethics.

(a) Identify whether the following statements about codes of ethics are true or false.

Statement	True ✓	False ✓
The AAT Code of Ethics is a rules-based code which details the specific procedures for every potential ethical dilemma.		
The AAT Code of Ethics sets out five fundamental principles of ethics.		

(2 marks)

You are an Accounting Technician assisting in the audit of Tanx Ltd, a new client for your audit firm. Your firm has never audited anyone in this industry before, although one of the team worked in the Tanx Ltd accounts department until last year. Your audit firm charged a low fee to Tanx Ltd in order to provide future consulting and tax services in the future.

The Finance Director of Tanx Ltd invited the team into their office and explained that if the audit could be done in a short timeframe with an unmodified report, they would offer the use of their corporate suite at the local football club for an upcoming game.

(b) Identify the most likely ethical threat and action that you should take for each situation.

Situation	Ethical threat	Action
Offering Tanx Ltd a low fee in order to win future work.	Gap 1	Action 1
The client offering the use of the corporate suite.	Gap 2	Action 2
One of the audit team used to work for Tanx Ltd.	Gap 3	Action 3

Gap 1	✓
Self-interest	
Intimidation	
Familiarity	

Gap 2	✓
Advocacy	
Self-review	
Self-interest	

Gap 3	✓
Self-Review	
Self-interest	
Advocacy	

Action 1	✓
Regular quality reviews	
Select smaller sample sizes	
Negotiate a bigger fee	

Action 2	✓
Accept the offer	
Reject the offer	
Resign	

Action 3	✓
Remove team member	
No changes	
Resign	

(6 marks)

(c) Identify which ONE of the following fundamental ethical principles is being threatened by auditing a client with a short timeframe in an industry that is unfamiliar to the company.

Ethical principle	✓
Professional behaviour	
Integrity	
Confidentiality	
Professional competence and due care	

(1 mark)

Your colleague has explained that they will audit trade payables and inventory, as they have worked on testing these areas before on a different client in an unrelated industry. You have also found out that the same colleague has begun a relationship with a member of the client staff who works in those areas.

(d) Identify whether the statements are true or false.

Statement	True ✓	False ✓
Your colleague should not audit these areas as they may breach confidentiality from another client.		
The relationship represents a familiarity threat to your colleague's objectivity.		
It would be illegal for your colleague to now continue on the audit team.		

(3 marks)

Your audit firm is now looking to tender for the audit for Linez Ltd, which is the main competitor of Tanx Ltd.

(e) Identify whether or not the following actions would be appropriate for your audit firm.

Action	Appropriate ✓	Not appropriate ✓
Disclose the potential audit engagement to both Tanx Ltd and Linez Ltd.		
Use the Tanx Ltd audit team on the Linez Ltd audit due to their experience in the industry.		
Arrange for both audit teams sign confidentiality agreements to ensure information is not passed between the teams.		

(3 marks)

MOCK ASSESSMENT QUESTIONS: SECTION 3

TASK 3 (25 MARKS)

This task is about the planning process.

(a) Identify whether the following statements present an inherent risk, detection risk or control risk.

Statement	Inherent Risk ✓	Detection Risk ✓	Control Risk ✓
The auditor will be using sampling within the audit.			
The client is in a highly regulated, complex industry.			
The Finance Controller and other key staff members left during the year.			

(3 marks)

(b) Identify whether the following statements are true or false.

Statement	True ✓	False ✓
Once set, materiality cannot be changed during an audit.		
All audit files must be shown to the client.		

(2 marks)

You are part of the audit team for the external audit of SciTech Ltd, a company that makes large medical testing equipment for laboratories and hospitals. These are often complex machines which can take a large number of months to construct. The audit manager has passed you details of what they know about SciTech's business during the year, which are shown below.

During the year ended 31 December 20X2 the company has been faced with a number of challenges. One of the largest selling products of SciTech Ltd, the CryoSpin, came under some criticism during the year due to a well-publicised situation involving the medical misdiagnosis of a celebrity figure. The celebrity successfully sued a medical clinic for £12 million. The clinic claims that the fault lies with the CryoSpin and is pursuing a case against SciTech Ltd.

As a response to this situation, demand for the CryoSpin has fallen. SciTech Ltd has been able to sell some of CryoSpin machines at a reduced price but has begun to construct and sell a new machine called CytoVac, which it hopes will be successful in eventually replacing the lost CryoSpin sales. SciTech Ltd has received a number of deposits from customers who have ordered the CytoVac. There have been some delays in the CytoVac production and SciTech Ltd has only been able to sell and install a small number of these before 31 December 20X2.

SciTech Ltd has also received notice that some customers who purchased CryoSpin machines are considering returning them if SciTech Ltd loses the court case. They are also refusing to pay the outstanding amounts owed until the court case is resolved. In addition to this, you have been made aware that there have been financial difficulties in the medical sector during the year with some clinics and laboratories being forced to cease operations.

Some preliminary figures from SciTech Ltd's financial statements are shown below.

	20X2 £000	20X1 £000
Revenue	142,400	137,500
Cost of sales	(74,520)	(77,600)
Gross profit	67,880	59,900
Inventories	45,300	34,600
Trade and other receivables	43,600	31,500
Provisions	3,600	3,400

(c) Using the information from the manager and the preliminary financial information:

   (i) Discuss THREE audit risks which should be considered when planning the audit of SciTech Ltd. **(12 marks)**

   (ii) For each risk identified in (i), explain the audit procedures to be performed.
   (8 marks)

Risk 1

Procedures for Risk 1

Risk 2

Procedures for Risk 2

Risk 3

Procedures for Risk 3

AAT: AUDIT AND ASSURANCE

TASK 4 (20 MARKS)

This task is about procedures for obtaining sufficient and appropriate audit evidence.

(a) Identify which of the following the auditor will be gaining assurance on by attending the inventory count. Select true or false for each option.

Statement	True ✓	False ✓
The existence of inventory.		
The effectiveness of the company's controls over the inventory count.		

(2 marks)

(b) Identify the type of sampling described below.

Description	Haphazard sampling ✓	Systematic sampling ✓	Monetary Unit Sampling ✓
Selecting 30 items without specific characteristic or bias.			
Selecting the balance every time the total crosses £10,000.			
The auditor selects every 10th balance.			

(3 marks)

(c) Identify whether the following statements are true or false.

Statement	True ✓	False ✓
Original documents are a better source of evidence than copies.		
Client-produced evidence is the most reliable source of evidence.		
Auditors only perform substantive procedures if controls are deficient.		

(3 marks)

You are assisting on the audit of Warm Ltd, a company that sells insulation to retailers and construction companies. A colleague of yours has been working on trade receivables and believes that their work is complete. They have asked you to look at their findings and see if you agree. Their notes are below.

Audit work on trade receivables

The sample size recommended by our audit firm's procedures was 25 customers. However, as Warm Ltd has many customers across Europe, I have excluded these. If these customers were removed from the list of balances it gives a sample size of 20, so I have selected 20 balances. One of these (R&F Ltd, £75,000) was the subject of a legal case so Sylvia, the Financial Controller asked me to pick another balance, which I did.

One balance (Blok Ltd, £60,000) was 30 days over its payment terms. Sylvia explained that this was common with this customer and therefore no further work is proposed.

One balance (Timb Ltd, £40,000) had a despatch note which showed that the goods were received in January 20X3. Sylvia tells me that Timb Ltd requested to be invoiced for this in December 20X2 for their own budget purposes.

One final balance (Hoam Ltd, £105,000) appeared to be misstated. A payment of £80,000 from Hoam Ltd was received in December but incorrectly applied to the balance of a different customer. As the overall balance of receivables was correct, no further work is proposed.

(d) Discuss the problems with the work carried out by your colleague and suggest some additional follow up procedures that they should perform. (10 marks)

Problems and suggested further procedures

Your role on the Warm Ltd audit is to examine the controls over the payroll function in the company. You have been given the following information about the payroll function from the payroll department.

When employees join Warm Ltd, they must fill in a joiners form and submit relevant ID so that their identity can be verified before paying them. Once these checks have been made, the form is sent to the Payroll Director for authorisation. If the Payroll Director is absent, another member of the board is able to authorise the employee for addition to the payroll.

(e) Suggest some tests of control which could be performed over the payroll process of adding employees to the payroll to ensure it is operating effectively. (2 marks)

Tests of control

TASK 5 (15 MARKS)

This task is about procedures for obtaining sufficient and appropriate audit evidence.

(a) **Complete the statement below:**

Auditors must gather sufficient appropriate evidence to support their audit opinion. Sufficiency relates to the _____GAP 1_____ of evidence whereas appropriate relates to the relevance and _____GAP 2_____ of evidence.

Gap 1	✓
reliability	
reasonableness	
quantity	

Gap 2	✓
reasonableness	
reliability	
quantity	

(2 marks)

(b) **Identify whether the following statements are true or false.**

Statement	True ✓	False ✓
Having an internal audit function forms part of the control environment of an entity.		
Auditors inspecting invoices for authorisation is a test of control.		
The client preparing monthly supplier reconciliations is a test of control.		

(3 marks)

You are an Accounting Technician assisting in the audit of the inventory of Flip Ltd. Flip Ltd is a manufacturer of sporting equipment, which it sells to both the general public via its website and to retailers. As Flip Ltd is a relatively new business, it rents some of its warehouse space to other companies to store goods in it.

(c) **Match the audit test to be performed over the inventory balance with the assertion they will provide evidence on.**

Test	Assertion
Selecting a sample of post year-end sales to ensure items sold above cost.	Picklist
Selecting a sample of goods in the warehouse and agreeing the purchase invoice stating that the goods belong to Flip Ltd.	Picklist
Examining the disclosures made and ensuring that the inventory balance is categorised between raw materials, work-in-progress and finished goods.	Picklist
Selecting a sample of goods from the inventory listing and tracing them to the warehouse floor.	Picklist

Options
Existence
Presentation
Rights and obligations
Valuation

(4 marks)

(d) Identify which TWO of the following substantive audit procedures provide the most appropriate evidence of the existence of trade receivables.

Procedure	✓
Selecting a sample of goods despatch notes signed by the customer as received.	
Selecting a sample of sales invoices sent to the client.	
Circularising a sample of trade receivable balances asking them to confirm the amounts owed to the client.	
Obtaining a breakdown of the receivables balance from the receivables ledger.	

(2 marks)

(e) Identify whether the following statements are true or false.

Statement	True ✓	False ✓
Test data is used to test the automated controls within a client's system.		
Data analytics allows auditors to test large quantities of data quickly.		
A photocopy is a better source of evidence than an original document.		
Analytical procedures should only be used during the evidence gathering stage of the audit.		

(4 marks)

TASK 6 (15 MARKS)

This task is about reviewing and reporting findings and audit opinions.

You are finishing the audit of Wails Ltd for the year ended 31 December 20X2. You have just discovered the news that Sute Ltd, a major customer of Wails Ltd has gone into liquidation. Upon further investigation, you have found out that Sute Ltd owed Wails Ltd a material amount at 31 December 20X2. As Sute Ltd had never previously missed any payments, this had not been identified as a risk in the audit testing done over trade receivables but you have since discovered that they had appointed administrators on 2 January 20X3.

Wails Ltd makes 50% of their sales to Sute Ltd. In addition to this, Wails Ltd has been using properties owned by Sute Ltd for its operations at a heavily discounted rate. These properties are now up for sale and it is unlikely that Wails Ltd will be able to continue to use them. The company is no longer a going concern but the Directors of Wails Ltd have prepared the financial statements on the going concern basis.

(a) **Explain the issues arising, any further work required and the potential impact on the audit report of Wails Ltd.** (10 marks)

Issues arising and impact on audit report

During the audit of Wails Ltd, you have noted a number of other situations that have arisen. Wails Ltd made a profit for the year of £600,000.

(b)   Identify the appropriate action in each of the following situations.

Situation	Do nothing ✓	Speak to manager ✓
During the inventory count, you noticed a small batch of damaged goods in the warehouse. After speaking to the Financial Controller, they have not written them down as they believe that they can sell them. They are valued at £3,000 in the financial statements.		
You have discovered an invoice for consulting services for £4,000. Upon investigation you have found that the consulting company is owned by the husband of the Finance Director. No disclosures have been made in the financial statements.		

(2 marks)

(c) Match the following statement with the opinions from the picklist below.

Statement	Opinion
The auditor does not express an opinion on the financial statements.	Picklist
The financial statements do not give a true and fair view.	Picklist
Except for the matter identified in the basis for modification paragraph, the financial statements give a true and fair view.	Picklist

Options
Qualified opinion
Disclaimer of opinion
Unmodified opinion
Adverse opinion

(3 marks)

Section 4

MOCK ASSESSMENT ANSWERS

TASK 1 (10 MARKS)

This task is about the conceptual and regulatory framework, corporate governance and internal audit.

(a) Identify whether the following statements about levels of assurance are true or false.

Statement	True ✓	False ✓
Reasonable assurance is always expressed with a positive conclusion.	✓	
Limited assurance can never be given.		✓

(2 marks)

(b) Identify which ONE of the following statements is correct in relation to internal audit.

Statement	✓
Having an internal audit function is a requirement for UK Listed Companies under the UK Corporate Governance Code so your audit report should identify this as inappropriate.	
If the board explain to shareholders why this decision has been made, it is in line with the UK Corporate Governance Code.	✓

(1 mark)

(c) Identify which TWO of the following are correct in respect of the UK Corporate Governance Code.

Statement	✓
The board of directors should establish procedures to minimise risk.	✓
The company should elect separate people as chairperson and chief executive.	✓
The board of directors should establish an Audit Committee with a minimum membership of five non-executive directors.	
All UK companies are required by law to comply with the code.	

(2 marks)

KAPLAN PUBLISHING

AAT: AUDIT AND ASSURANCE

(d) Identify the correct option for each responsibility.

Responsibility	Options
Preparation of the financial statements.	Board of directors
Ensure auditor recommendations are actioned.	Audit committee
Produce a report on whether the financial statements give a true and fair view.	External auditor

(3 marks)

(e) Complete the following statement:

An external audit gives _____GAP 1_____ assurance that the financial statements are true and fair, which means that they are free from _____GAP 2_____ misstatement, whether due to fraud or error.

Gap 1	✓
absolute	
reasonable	✓
limited	

Gap 2	✓
all	
major	
material	✓

(2 marks)

TASK 2 (15 MARKS)

This task is about professional ethics.

(a) Identify whether the following statements about codes of ethics are true or false.

Statement	True ✓	False ✓
The AAT Code of Ethics is a rules-based code which details the specific procedures for every potential ethical dilemma.		✓
The AAT Code of Ethics sets out five fundamental principles of ethics.	✓	

(2 marks)

(b) Identify the ethical threat and action that you should take for each situation.

Situation	Ethical threat	Action
Offering Tanx Ltd a low fee in order to win future work.	Gap 1	Action 1
The client offering the use of the corporate suite.	Gap 2	Action 2
One of the audit team used to work for Tanx Ltd.	Gap 3	Action 3

Gap 1	✓
Self-interest	✓
Intimidation	
Familiarity	

Gap 2	✓
Advocacy	
Self-review	
Self-interest	✓

Gap 3	✓
Self-review	✓
Self-interest	
Advocacy	

MOCK ASSESSMENT ANSWERS: SECTION 4

Action 1	✓
Regular quality reviews	✓
Select smaller sample sizes	
Negotiate a bigger fee	

Action 2	✓
Accept the offer	
Reject the offer	✓
Resign	

Action 3	✓
Remove team member	✓
No changes	
Resign	

(6 marks)

(c) Identify which ONE of the following fundamental ethical principles is being threatened by auditing a client with a short timeframe in an industry that is unfamiliar to the company.

Ethical principle	✓
Professional behaviour	
Integrity	
Confidentiality	
Professional competence and due care	✓

(1 mark)

(d) Identify whether the statements are true or false.

Statement	True ✓	False ✓
Your colleague should not audit these areas as they may breach confidentiality from another client.		✓
The relationship represents a familiarity threat to your colleague's objectivity.	✓	
It would be illegal for your colleague to now continue on the audit team.		✓

(3 marks)

(e) Identify whether or not the following actions would be appropriate for your audit firm.

Action	Appropriate ✓	Not appropriate ✓
Disclose the potential audit engagement to both Tanx Ltd and Linez Ltd.	✓	
Use the Tanx Ltd audit team on the Linez Ltd audit due to their experience in the industry.		✓
Arrange for both audit teams sign confidentiality agreements to ensure information is not passed between the teams.	✓	

(3 marks)

TASK 3 (25 MARKS)

This task is about the planning process.

(a) Identify whether the following statements present an inherent risk, detection risk or control risk.

Statement	Inherent Risk ✓	Detection Risk ✓	Control Risk ✓
The auditor will be using sampling within the audit.		✓	
The client is in a highly regulated, complex industry.	✓		
The Finance Controller and other key staff members left during the year.			✓

(3 marks)

(b) Identify whether the following statements are true or false.

Statement	True ✓	False ✓
Once set, materiality cannot be changed during an audit.		✓
All audit files must be shown to the client.		✓

(2 marks)

(c) (i) Discuss THREE audit risks which should be considered when planning the audit of SciTech Ltd. **(12 marks)**

(ii) For each risk identified in (i), explain the audit procedures to be performed. **(8 marks)**

Risks
Indicative content (1 mark per point). Only three risks are required and only three should be marked, but there are four issues that could be discussed.
Risk 1 (max 4 marks):
• The court case with a celebrity could mean that liabilities in SciTech Ltd are understated.
• A provision should be recorded by SciTech Ltd if it is probable that they will lose the court case from the medical facility.
• Looking at the financial statements, there has been no significant increase in provisions so it appears this is not recorded.
• There is the potential that the court case could cause doubt over SciTech Ltd's ability to continue as a going concern. This could either be due to the potentially large settlement required or to the loss of custom from customers returning machines or refusing to pay.
• If SciTech Ltd is no longer a going concern, then the accounts would need to be prepared on a break-up basis, with all assets and liabilities being current and all assets held at their sale values.

MOCK ASSESSMENT ANSWERS: SECTION 4

Procedures for risk 1 (max 3 marks):

- Enquire with the SciTech Ltd legal team in order to examine the recent progress of the court case.
- Enquire with an independent legal expert about the likely outcome of the case.
- Inspect publicly available documents from the celebrity case to see if the cause of the failure was the machine.
- Examine correspondence from customers that are refusing to pay in order to assess if legal action will be taken if they continue to refuse.
- Enquire whether any customers have since paid SciTech Ltd.

Risk 2 (max 4 marks):

- Revenue may have been recognised on the new machines too early.
- Revenue should only be recognised when the machines are delivered, not when the deposits are received.
- There is an increase in revenue despite the loss of custom from the CryoSpin, which raises the possibility of an error in recognising revenue.
- This may mean that the cut-off procedures in relation to revenue are incorrect, with items being included in revenue and in inventory.
- This is further supported by an increase in gross profit margin from 43.6% to 47.6% which could be the result of recognising revenue before any costs have been included in cost of sales.

Procedures for risk 2 (max 3 marks):

- Obtain a list of sales recorded for the new machines and compare the list to items delivered before the year-end.
- Obtain a list of inventory to ensure no items are included in revenue and inventory.
- Once this has been discussed, examine the reasons for the increase in revenue with management.
- Obtain information regarding returns after the year-end to see if some of the CryoSpin's have been returned and need to be removed from revenue.

Risk 3 (max 4 marks):

- There is a risk that receivables may be overstated in the financial statements.
- This is supported by an increase in receivables collection period from 84 days to 112 days.
- This risk may be due to sales being recognised too early on the new machines if the full sale is being recognised before despatch.
- The receivables may also be overstated due to some outstanding balances not being paid following the CryoSpin issue.
- There are also concerns over the recoverability of amounts following financial problems in the sector.

KAPLAN PUBLISHING

Procedures for risk 3 (max 3 marks):

- Inspect the aged receivables ledger to assess if any balances appear significantly over their payment terms.
- For any overdue balances, inspect correspondence with the customer to see if they have registered a complaint following the CryoSpin issue.
- Inspect publicly available documentation regarding outstanding balances to see if any customers have declared financial problems.
- Enquire with management to assess any ongoing discussions with outstanding customers.
- If sales of the new machine have been recognised before despatch, ensure the outstanding receivable is reversed as well as the deposit received.
- For any new customers in the year, obtain details of any credit checks performed.
- Ascertain whether any payments have been received from receivables after the year-end.

Risk 4 (max 4 marks):

- Inventory could be overstated due to the problems with the CryoSpin.
- Inventory turnover period has increased from 163 days to 222 days which could suggest that there is a high amount of CryoSpin which cannot be sold.
- As some CryoSpin machines have been sold at a discount, there is a risk that inventory has a lower NRV than the cost and needs to be written down.
- Inventory for the new machines could be classed as work-in-progress, which could be difficult to assess in terms of value due to the complex nature of the machines.
- Inventory may be understated if customers have since sent back CryoSpin machines following the criticism.

Procedures for risk 4 (max 3 marks):

- Consider employing an expert to review the status of any work-in-progress due to its technical nature.
- Examine if any CryoSpin machines have been sold post year-end below cost.
- Examine if any CryoSpin machines were returned post year-end and need to be included within inventory.

MOCK ASSESSMENT ANSWERS: SECTION 4

TASK 4 (20 MARKS)

This task is about procedures for obtaining sufficient and appropriate audit evidence.

(a) Identify which of the following the auditor will be gaining assurance on by attending the inventory count. Select true or false for each option.

Statement	True ✓	False ✓
The existence of inventory.	✓	
The effectiveness of the company's controls over the inventory count.	✓	

(2 marks)

(b) Identify the type of sampling identified below

Description	Haphazard sampling ✓	Systematic sampling ✓	Monetary Unit sampling ✓
Selecting 30 items without specific characteristic or bias.	✓		
Selecting the balance every time the total crosses £10,000.			✓
The auditor selects every 10th balance.		✓	

(3 marks)

(c) Identify whether the statements below are true or false

Statement	True ✓	False ✓
Original documents are a better source of evidence than copies.	✓	
Client-produced evidence is the most reliable source of evidence.		✓
Auditors only perform substantive procedures if controls are deficient.		✓

(3 marks)

(d) Discuss the problems with the work carried out by your colleague and suggest some additional follow up procedures that they should perform. **(10 marks)**

Problems and suggested further procedures
Indicative content (1 mark per identified problem and 1 mark per identified action)
• European items have been excluded from the sample. These could present higher risk of misstatement due to potential translation issues and delivery times.
• A sample has been selected which is smaller than the firm's policy so could increase the risk of not detecting material misstatements.

KAPLAN PUBLISHING

- One of the items in the sample has been changed at the client's request. This is a problem as the balance could contain a fraud or error and the client could be hiding this.
- One balance is overdue (Blok Ltd). The explanation from Sylvia may be correct but your colleague needs to make further enquiries to corroborate this.
- The sale to Timb Ltd appears to have been in 20X3 so should not be recognised as a sale during the year, meaning that revenue and receivables are overstated. Your colleague should recommend that this is corrected. Even though this is not individually material, there could be other transactions like this.
- This misposting could result in other inaccurate receivables balances. This may mean the total is not misstated but could lead to problems over the collection of some items if Warm Ltd does not know the correct amounts owed from each customer.
- Overall, your colleague appears too trusting of the client responses and has not sought to obtain sufficient evidence to corroborate the explanation or confirm the outstanding balance.
- There are a number of material errors in the sample and your colleague has not proposed any further work over receivables.

Action to be taken:

- Increase the sample size selected so it is in line with the firm's policies.
- Select some European balances to test as these carry a different risk to the UK-based ones.
- Ensure R&F Ltd is included in the balance and inspect the documentation surrounding the dispute.
- Inspect correspondence from R&F Ltd as it could suggest the balance is not recoverable.
- Inspect the history of payments from Blok Ltd to assess if they have a history of paying late to corroborate Sylvie's explanation.
- Enquire as to whether Blok Ltd pay the balance prior to the completion of the audit.
- Select a sample of January despatch notes to see if there are other items like the sale to Timb Ltd which suggest an overstatement of revenue and receivables.
- Enquire as to whether there are any other instances of misallocated payments perhaps by looking for balances with a credit balance or any large overdue amounts.
- Due to the large number of issues noted, it is suggested that your colleague extends the sample as it appears that the balance is materially misstated.

(e) (2 marks)

Tests of control
Indicative content (1 mark per well-explained test of control)

- Select a sample of individuals and inspect evidence of a valid form of ID held on file.
- Select a sample from the joiners in the year and inspect their completed joiner form.
- Seek evidence of authorisation on the joiner form from the Payroll Director or other board member.

TASK 5 (15 MARKS)

This task is about procedures for obtaining sufficient and appropriate audit evidence.

(a) **Complete the statement below:**

Auditors must gather sufficient appropriate evidence to support their audit opinion. Sufficiency relates to the _____GAP 1_____ of evidence whereas appropriate relates to the relevance and _____GAP 2_____ of evidence.

Gap 1	✓
reliability	
reasonableness	
quantity	✓

Gap 2	✓
reasonableness	
reliability	✓
quantity	

(2 marks)

(b) **Identify whether the following statements are true or false.**

Statements	True ✓	False ✓
Having an internal audit function forms part of the control environment of an entity.	✓	
Auditors inspecting invoices for authorisation is a test of control.	✓	
The client preparing monthly supplier reconciliations is a test of control.		✓

(3 marks)

(c) **Match the audit test to be performed over the inventory balance with the assertion they will provide evidence on.**

Test	Assertion
Selecting a sample of post year-end sales to ensure items sold above cost.	Valuation
Selecting a sample of goods in the warehouse and agreeing purchase invoice stating that the goods belong to Flip Ltd.	Rights and obligations
Examining the disclosures made and ensuring that the inventory balance is categorised between raw materials, work-in-progress and finished goods.	Presentation
Selecting a sample of goods from the inventory listing and tracing them to the warehouse floor.	Existence

(4 marks)

(d) Identify which TWO of the following substantive audit procedures provide the most appropriate evidence of the existence of trade receivables.

Procedure	✓
Selecting a sample of goods despatch notes signed by the customer as received.	✓
Selecting a sample of sales invoices sent to the client.	
Circularising a sample of trade receivable balances asking them to confirm the amounts owed to the client.	✓
Obtaining a breakdown of the receivables balance from the sales ledger.	

(2 marks)

(e) Identify whether the following statements are true or false.

Statement	True ✓	False ✓
Test data is used to test the automated controls within a client's system.	✓	
Data analytics allows auditors to test large quantities of data quickly.	✓	
A photocopy is a better source of evidence than an original document.		✓
Analytical procedures should only be used during the evidence gathering stage of the audit.		✓

(4 marks)

Further to the AAT's announcement of the change in mark allocation within the Audit and Assurance assessment, we have provided updated mocks to replace those previously published within our bound books.

The updated Mock Assessment reflects the exam format for live assessments from 16 September 2024 onwards. From this date, the AAT AUDT exam will consist of 30% human-marked requirements and 70% computer-marked requirements.

Section 3

MOCK ASSESSMENT QUESTIONS

The assessment is 2.5 hours long and consists of 6 tasks. You should attempt all of the tasks. Each task is independent and you will not need to refer to previous tasks.

TASK 1 (10 MARKS)

This task is about the conceptual and regulatory framework, corporate governance and internal audit.

(a) **Identify whether the following statements about levels of assurance are true or false.**

Statement	True ✓	False ✓
Reasonable assurance is always expressed with a positive conclusion.		
Limited assurance can never be given.		

(2 marks)

(b) You are the external auditor of a company whose board have decided to disband their internal audit team, and have given you reasons for doing so.

Identify which ONE of the following statements is correct in relation to internal audit.

Statement	✓
Having an internal audit function is a requirement for UK Listed Companies under the UK Corporate Governance Code so your audit report should identify this as inappropriate.	
If the board explain to shareholders why this decision has been made, it is in line with the UK Corporate Governance Code.	

(1 mark)

(c) Identify which TWO of the following are correct in respect of the UK Corporate Governance Code.

Statement	✓
The board of directors should establish procedures to minimise risk.	
The company should elect separate people as chairperson and chief executive.	
The board of directors should establish an Audit Committee with a minimum membership of five non-executive directors.	
All UK companies are required by law to comply with the code.	

(2 marks)

(d) Identify the correct option for each responsibility.

Responsibility	Options
Preparation of the financial statements.	PICKLIST
Ensure auditor recommendations are actioned.	PICKLIST
Produce a report on whether the financial statements give a true and fair view.	PICKLIST

Options
External auditors
Board of directors
Audit committee
Internal auditors

(3 marks)

(e) Complete the following statement about the auditing process:

An external audit gives ____GAP 1_____ assurance that the financial statements are true and fair, which means that they are free from _____GAP 2_____ misstatement, whether due to fraud or error.

Gap 1	✓
absolute	
reasonable	
limited	

Gap 2	✓
all	
major	
material	

(2 marks)

TASK 2 (15 MARKS)

This task is about professional ethics.

(a) Identify whether the following statements about codes of ethics are true or false.

Statement	True ✓	False ✓
The AAT Code of Ethics is a rules-based code which details the specific procedures for every potential ethical dilemma.		
The AAT Code of Ethics sets out five fundamental principles of ethics.		

(2 marks)

You are an Accounting Technician assisting in the audit of Tanx Ltd, a new client for your audit firm. Your firm has never audited anyone in this industry before, although one of the team worked in the Tanx Ltd accounts department until last year. Your audit firm charged a low fee to Tanx Ltd in order to provide future consulting and tax services in the future.

The Finance Director of Tanx Ltd invited the team into their office and explained that if the audit could be done in a short timeframe with an unmodified report, they would offer the use of their corporate suite at the local football club for an upcoming game.

(b) Identify the most likely ethical threat and action that you should take for each situation.

Situation	Ethical threat	Action
Offering Tanx Ltd a low fee in order to win future work.	Gap 1	Action 1
The client offering the use of the corporate suite.	Gap 2	Action 2
One of the audit team used to work for Tanx Ltd.	Gap 3	Action 3

Gap 1	✓
Self-interest	
Intimidation	
Familiarity	

Gap 2	✓
Advocacy	
Self-review	
Self-interest	

Gap 3	✓
Self-Review	
Self-interest	
Advocacy	

Action 1	✓
Regular quality reviews	
Select smaller sample sizes	
Negotiate a bigger fee	

Action 2	✓
Accept the offer	
Reject the offer	
Resign	

Action 3	✓
Remove team member	
No changes	
Resign	

(6 marks)

(c) Identify which ONE of the following fundamental ethical principles is being threatened by auditing a client with a short timeframe in an industry that is unfamiliar to the company.

Ethical principle	✓
Professional behaviour	
Integrity	
Confidentiality	
Professional competence and due care	

(1 mark)

Your colleague has explained that they will audit trade payables and inventory, as they have worked on testing these areas before on a different client in an unrelated industry. You have also found out that the same colleague has begun a relationship with a member of the client staff who works in those areas.

(d) Identify whether the statements are true or false.

Statement	True ✓	False ✓
Your colleague should not audit these areas as they may breach confidentiality from another client.		
The relationship represents a familiarity threat to your colleague's objectivity.		
It would be illegal for your colleague to now continue on the audit team.		

(3 marks)

Your audit firm is now looking to tender for the audit for Linez Ltd, which is the main competitor of Tanx Ltd.

(e) Identify whether or not the following actions would be appropriate for your audit firm.

Action	Appropriate ✓	Not appropriate ✓
Disclose the potential audit engagement to both Tanx Ltd and Linez Ltd.		
Use the Tanx Ltd audit team on the Linez Ltd audit due to their experience in the industry.		
Arrange for both audit teams sign confidentiality agreements to ensure information is not passed between the teams.		

(3 marks)

MOCK ASSESSMENT QUESTIONS: SECTION 3

TASK 3 (25 MARKS)

This task is about the planning process.

(a) Identify whether the following statements present an inherent risk, detection risk or control risk.

Statement	Inherent Risk ✓	Detection Risk ✓	Control Risk ✓
The auditor will be using sampling within the audit.			
The client is in a highly regulated, complex industry.			
The Finance Controller and other key staff members left during the year.			

(3 marks)

(b) Identify whether the following statements are true or false.

Statement	True ✓	False ✓
Once set, materiality cannot be changed during an audit.		
All audit files must be shown to the client.		

(2 marks)

You are part of the audit team for the external audit of SciTech Ltd, a company that makes large medical testing equipment for laboratories and hospitals. These are often complex machines which can take a large number of months to construct. The audit manager has passed you details of what they know about SciTech's business during the year, which are shown below.

> During the year ended 31 December 20X2 the company has been faced with a number of challenges. One of the largest selling products of SciTech Ltd, the CryoSpin, came under some criticism during the year due to a well-publicised situation involving the medical misdiagnosis of a celebrity figure. The celebrity successfully sued a medical clinic for £12 million. The clinic claims that the fault lies with the CryoSpin and is pursuing a case against SciTech Ltd.
>
> As a response to this situation, demand for the CryoSpin has fallen. SciTech Ltd has been able to sell some of CryoSpin machines at a reduced price but has begun to construct and sell a new machine called CytoVac, which it hopes will be successful in eventually replacing the lost CryoSpin sales. SciTech Ltd has received a number of deposits from customers who have ordered the CytoVac. There have been some delays in the CytoVac production and SciTech Ltd has only been able to sell and install a small number of these before 31 December 20X2.
>
> SciTech Ltd has also received notice that some customers who purchased CryoSpin machines are considering returning them if SciTech Ltd loses the court case. They are also refusing to pay the outstanding amounts owed until the court case is resolved. In addition to this, you have been made aware that there have been financial difficulties in the medical sector during the year with some clinics and laboratories being forced to cease operations.

AAT: **AUDIT AND ASSURANCE**

Some preliminary figures from SciTech Ltd's financial statements are shown below.

	20X2 £000	20X1 £000
Revenue	142,400	137,500
Cost of sales	(74,520)	(77,600)
Gross profit	67,880	59,900
Inventories	45,300	34,600
Trade and other receivables	43,600	31,500
Provisions	3,600	3,400

The Audit Partner decided that materiality should be 0.4% of revenue, rounded down to the nearest £1,000.

(c) (i) **Identify the correct materiality calculated using the Audit Partner's instructions.**
 (1 mark)

 Materiality is £ ☐

 To assist the External Audit Partner in preparation for planning the audit of SciTech Ltd:

 (ii) **Explain THREE areas of audit risk that could have a potential impact on the financial statements. Include reference to analytical procedures as part of your answer if appropriate.** **(6 marks)**

 (iii) **Describe the audit procedures and other steps that should be undertaken to reduce EACH risk identified above to an acceptable level.** **(6 marks)**

Risk 1

Procedures for Risk 1

Risk 2

Procedures for Risk 2

Risk 3

Procedures for Risk 3

(d) Identify whether each of the following documents should be kept in the Permanent Audit Files (PAF) or the Current Audit Files (CAF).

Document	PAF ✓	CAF ✓
Current year bank statements		
Articles of incorporation		
Lease agreements		

(3 marks)

(e) Identify whether the following statements about recording techniques are true or false.

Statement	True ✓	False ✓
Narrative notes offer detailed explanations of internal controls.		
Questionnaires allow for comprehensive details about internal controls.		
Flowcharts are suitable for both simple and complex processes.		
Questionnaires are generally quicker to prepare and administer than narrative notes and flowcharts.		

(4 marks)

MOCK ASSESSMENT QUESTIONS: SECTION 3

TASK 4 (20 MARKS)

This task is about procedures for obtaining sufficient and appropriate audit evidence.

(a) Identify which of the following the auditor will be gaining assurance on by attending the inventory count. Select true or false for each option.

Statement	True ✓	False ✓
The existence of inventory.		
The effectiveness of the company's controls over the inventory count.		

(2 marks)

(b) Identify the type of sampling described below.

Description	Haphazard ✓	Systematic ✓	Monetary Unit Sampling ✓
Selecting 30 items without specific characteristic or bias.			
Selecting the balance every time the total crosses £10,000.			
The auditor selects every 10th balance.			

(3 marks)

(c) Identify whether the following statements are true or false.

Statement	True ✓	False ✓
Original documents are a better source of evidence than copies.		
Client-produced evidence is the most reliable source of evidence.		
Auditors only perform substantive procedures if controls are deficient.		

(3 marks)

You are assisting on the audit of Warm Ltd, a company that sells insulation to retailers and construction companies. A colleague of yours has been working on trade receivables and believes that their work is complete. They have asked you to look at their findings and see if you agree. Their notes are below.

Audit work on trade receivables

The sample size recommended by our audit firm's procedures was 25 customers. However, as Warm Ltd has many customers across Europe, I have excluded these. If these customers were removed from the list of balances it gives a sample size of 20, so I have selected 20 balances. One of these (R&F Ltd, £75,000) was the subject of a legal case so Sylvia, the Financial Controller asked me to pick another balance, which I did.

One balance (Blok Ltd, £60,000) was 30 days over its payment terms. Sylvia explained that this was common with this customer and therefore no further work is proposed.

One balance (Timb Ltd, £40,000) had a despatch note which showed that the goods were received in January 20X3. Sylvia tells me that Timb Ltd requested to be invoiced for this in December 20X2 for their own budget purposes.

One final balance (Hoam Ltd, £105,000) appeared to be misstated. A payment of £80,000 from Hoam Ltd was received in December but incorrectly applied to the balance of a different customer. As the overall balance of receivables was correct, no further work is proposed.

(d) **(i)** Discuss THREE problems with the work carried out by your colleague. (3 marks)

(ii) Suggest TWO additional follow up procedures that they should perform. (2 marks)

Problems

Suggested follow up procedures

MOCK ASSESSMENT QUESTIONS: **SECTION 3**

Your role on the Warm Ltd audit is to examine the controls over the payroll function in the company. You have been given the following information about the payroll function from the payroll department.

When employees join Warm Ltd, they must fill in a joiners form and submit relevant ID so that their identity can be verified before paying them. Once these checks have been made, the form is sent to the Payroll Director for authorisation. If the Payroll Director is absent, another member of the board is able to authorise the employee for addition to the payroll.

(e) **Explain TWO tests of control which could be performed over the payroll process of adding employees to the payroll to ensure it is operating effectively.**

When asked to explain, students are expected to state the procedure and the audit objective of the procedure. **(4 marks)**

Tests of control

(f) Match the statement with the type of internal control it is describing.

Internal control	Assertion
Conducting monthly reconciliations of bank statements.	Picklist
Employee A reviews and approves the invoice. Employee B records the approved invoice in the accounting system. Employee C processes the payment for the recorded invoice.	Picklist
Using software to monitor and log access to sensitive data by employees.	Picklist

Options
A preventative control
A detective control

(3 marks)

TASK 5 (15 MARKS)

This task is about procedures for obtaining sufficient and appropriate audit evidence.

(a) **Complete the following statement about evidence gathering:**

Auditors must gather sufficient appropriate evidence to support their audit opinion. Sufficiency relates to the ____GAP 1_____ of evidence whereas appropriate relates to the relevance and _____GAP 2_____ of evidence.

Gap 1	✓
reliability	
reasonableness	
quantity	

Gap 2	✓
reasonableness	
reliability	
quantity	

(2 marks)

(b) **Identify whether the following statements are true or false.**

Statement	True ✓	False ✓
Having an internal audit function forms part of the control environment of an entity.		
Auditors inspecting invoices for authorisation is a test of control.		
The client preparing monthly supplier reconciliations is a test of control.		

(3 marks)

You are an Accounting Technician assisting in the audit of the inventory of Flip Ltd. Flip Ltd is a manufacturer of sporting equipment, which it sells to both the general public via its website and to retailers. As Flip Ltd is a relatively new business, it rents some of its warehouse space to other companies to store goods in it.

(c) **Match the audit test to be performed over the inventory balance with the assertion they will provide evidence on.**

Test	Assertion
Selecting a sample of post year-end sales to ensure items sold above cost.	Picklist
Selecting a sample of goods in the warehouse and agreeing the purchase invoice stating that the goods belong to Flip Ltd.	Picklist
Examining the disclosures made and ensuring that the inventory balance is categorised between raw materials, work-in-progress and finished goods.	Picklist
Selecting a sample of goods from the inventory listing and tracing them to the warehouse floor.	Picklist

Options
Existence
Presentation
Rights and obligations
Valuation

(4 marks)

(d) **Identify which TWO of the following substantive audit procedures provide the most appropriate evidence of the existence of trade receivables.**

Procedure	✓
Selecting a sample of goods despatch notes signed by the customer as received.	
Selecting a sample of sales invoices sent to the client.	
Circularising a sample of trade receivable balances asking them to confirm the amounts owed to the client.	
Obtaining a breakdown of the receivables balance from the receivables ledger.	

(2 marks)

(e) **Identify whether the following statements are true or false.**

Statement	True ✓	False ✓
Test data is used to test the automated controls within a client's system.		
Data analytics allows auditors to test large quantities of data quickly.		
A photocopy is a better source of evidence than an original document.		
Analytical procedures should only be used during the evidence gathering stage of the audit.		

(4 marks)

AAT: AUDIT AND ASSURANCE

TASK 6 (15 MARKS)

This task is about reviewing and reporting findings and audit opinions.

You are finishing the audit of Wails Ltd for the year ended 31 December 20X2. You have just discovered the news that Sute Ltd, a major customer of Wails Ltd has gone into liquidation. Upon further investigation, you have found out that Sute Ltd owed Wails Ltd a material amount at 31 December 20X2. As Sute Ltd had never previously missed any payments, this had not been identified as a risk in the audit testing done over trade receivables but you have since discovered that they had appointed administrators on 2 January 20X3.

Wails Ltd makes 50% of their sales to Sute Ltd. In addition to this, Wails Ltd has been using properties owned by Sute Ltd for its operations at a heavily discounted rate. These properties are now up for sale and it is unlikely that Wails Ltd will be able to continue to use them. The company is no longer a going concern but the Directors of Wails Ltd have prepared the financial statements on the going concern basis.

(a) Explain the issues arising, any further work required and the potential impact on the audit report of Wails Ltd. **(9 marks)**

Issues arising and impact on audit report

During the audit of Wails Ltd, you have noted a number of other situations that have arisen. Wails Ltd made a profit for the year of £600,000.

(b) **Identify the appropriate action in each of the following situations.**

Situation	Do nothing ✓	Speak to manager ✓
During the inventory count, you noticed a small batch of damaged goods in the warehouse. After speaking to the Financial Controller, they have not written them down as they believe that they can sell them. They are valued at £3,000 in the financial statements.		
You have discovered an invoice for consulting services for £4,000. Upon investigation you have found that the consulting company is owned by the husband of the Finance Director. No disclosures have been made in the financial statements.		

(2 marks)

AAT: AUDIT AND ASSURANCE

(c) Match the following statement with the opinions from the picklist below.

Statement	Opinion
The auditor does not express an opinion on the financial statements.	Picklist
The financial statements do not give a true and fair view.	Picklist
Except for the matter identified in the basis for modification paragraph, the financial statements give a true and fair view.	Picklist

Options
Qualified opinion
Disclaimer of opinion
Unmodified opinion
Adverse opinion

(3 marks)

(d) Identify whether the following statement is true or false.

Statement	True ✓	False ✓
A modified audit report always means that the opinion is modified.		

(1 mark)

Section 4

MOCK ASSESSMENT ANSWERS

TASK 1 (10 MARKS)

This task is about the conceptual and regulatory framework, corporate governance and internal audit.

(a) Identify whether the following statements about levels of assurance are true or false.

Statement	True ✓	False ✓
Reasonable assurance is always expressed with a positive conclusion.	✓	
Limited assurance can never be given.		✓

(2 marks)

(b) Identify which ONE of the following statements is correct in relation to internal audit.

Statement	✓
Having an internal audit function is a requirement for UK Listed Companies under the UK Corporate Governance Code so your audit report should identify this as inappropriate.	
If the board explain to shareholders why this decision has been made, it is in line with the UK Corporate Governance Code.	✓

(1 mark)

(c) Identify which TWO of the following are correct in respect of the UK Corporate Governance Code.

Statement	✓
The board of directors should establish procedures to minimise risk.	✓
The company should elect separate people as chairperson and chief executive.	✓
The board of directors should establish an Audit Committee with a minimum membership of five non-executive directors.	
All UK companies are required by law to comply with the code.	

(2 marks)

AAT: AUDIT AND ASSURANCE

(d) Identify the correct option for each responsibility.

Responsibility	Options
Preparation of the financial statements.	Board of directors
Ensure auditor recommendations are actioned.	Audit committee
Produce a report on whether the financial statements give a true and fair view.	External auditor

(3 marks)

(e) Complete the following statement about the auditing process:

An external audit gives ____GAP 1_____ assurance that the financial statements are true and fair, which means that they are free from _____GAP 2_____ misstatement, whether due to fraud or error.

Gap 1	✓
absolute	
reasonable	✓
limited	

Gap 2	✓
all	
major	
material	✓

(2 marks)

TASK 2 (15 MARKS)

This task is about professional ethics.

(a) Identify whether the following statements about codes of ethics are true or false.

Statement	True ✓	False ✓
The AAT Code of Ethics is a rules-based code which details the specific procedures for every potential ethical dilemma.		✓
The AAT Code of Ethics sets out five fundamental principles of ethics.	✓	

(2 marks)

(b) Identify the ethical threat and action that you should take for each situation.

Situation	Ethical threat	Action
Offering Tanx Ltd a low fee in order to win future work.	Gap 1	Action 1
The client offering the use of the corporate suite.	Gap 2	Action 2
One of the audit team used to work for Tanx Ltd.	Gap 3	Action 3

Gap 1	✓
Self-interest	✓
Intimidation	
Familiarity	

Gap 2	✓
Advocacy	
Self-review	
Self-interest	✓

Gap 3	✓
Self-review	✓
Self-interest	
Advocacy	

MOCK ASSESSMENT ANSWERS: SECTION 4

Action 1	✓
Regular quality reviews	✓
Select smaller sample sizes	
Negotiate a bigger fee	

Action 2	✓
Accept the offer	
Reject the offer	✓
Resign	

Action 3	✓
Remove team member	✓
No changes	
Resign	

(6 marks)

(c) Identify which ONE of the following fundamental ethical principles is being threatened by auditing a client with a short timeframe in an industry that is unfamiliar to the company.

Ethical principle	✓
Professional behaviour	
Integrity	
Confidentiality	
Professional competence and due care	✓

(1 mark)

(d) Identify whether the statements are true or false.

Statement	True ✓	False ✓
Your colleague should not audit these areas as they may breach confidentiality from another client.		✓
The relationship represents a familiarity threat to your colleague's objectivity.	✓	
It would be illegal for your colleague to now continue on the audit team.		✓

(3 marks)

(e) Identify whether or not the following actions would be appropriate for your audit firm.

Action	Appropriate ✓	Not appropriate ✓
Disclose the potential audit engagement to both Tanx Ltd and Linez Ltd.	✓	
Use the Tanx Ltd audit team on the Linez Ltd audit due to their experience in the industry.		✓
Arrange for both audit teams sign confidentiality agreements to ensure information is not passed between the teams.	✓	

(3 marks)

KAPLAN PUBLISHING

AAT: AUDIT AND ASSURANCE

TASK 3 (25 MARKS)

This task is about the planning process.

(a) Identify whether the following statements present an inherent risk, detection risk or control risk.

Statement	Inherent Risk ✓	Detection Risk ✓	Control Risk ✓
The auditor will be using sampling within the audit.		✓	
The client is in a highly regulated, complex industry.	✓		
The Finance Controller and other key staff members left during the year.			✓

(3 marks)

(b) Identify whether the following statements are true or false.

Statement	True ✓	False ✓
Once set, materiality cannot be changed during an audit.		✓
All audit files must be shown to the client.		✓

(2 marks)

(c) (i) Identify the correct materiality calculated using the Audit Partner's instructions.

(1 mark)

Materiality is £ 569,000

To assist the External Audit Partner in preparation for planning the audit of SciTech Ltd:

(ii) Explain THREE areas of audit risk that could have a potential impact on the financial statements. Include reference to analytical procedures as part of your answer if appropriate. (6 marks)

(iii) Describe the audit procedures that should be undertaken to reduce EACH risk identified above to an acceptable level. (6 marks)

Risks
Indicative content (1 mark per point). Only three risks are required and only three should be marked, but there are four issues that could be discussed.
Risk 1 (max 2 marks):
• The court case with a celebrity could mean that liabilities in SciTech Ltd are understated.
• A provision should be recorded by SciTech Ltd if it is probable that they will lose the court case from the medical facility.
• Looking at the financial statements, there has been no significant increase in provisions so it appears this is not recorded.

- There is the potential that the court case could cause doubt over SciTech Ltd's ability to continue as a going concern. This could either be due to the potentially large settlement required or to the loss of custom from customers returning machines or refusing to pay.
- If SciTech Ltd is no longer a going concern, then the accounts would need to be prepared on a break-up basis, with all assets and liabilities being current and all assets held at their sale values.

Procedures for risk 1 (max 2 marks):

- Enquire with the SciTech Ltd legal team in order to examine the recent progress of the court case.
- Enquire with an independent legal expert about the likely outcome of the case.
- Inspect publicly available documents from the celebrity case to see if the cause of the failure was the machine.
- Examine correspondence from customers that are refusing to pay in order to assess if legal action will be taken if they continue to refuse.
- Enquire whether any customers have since paid SciTech Ltd.

Risk 2 (max 2 marks):

- Revenue may have been recognised on the new machines too early.
- Revenue should only be recognised when the machines are delivered, not when the deposits are received.
- There is an increase in revenue despite the loss of custom from the CryoSpin, which raises the possibility of an error in recognising revenue.
- This may mean that the cut-off procedures in relation to revenue are incorrect, with items being included in revenue and in inventory.
- This is further supported by an increase in gross profit margin from 43.6% to 47.6% which could be the result of recognising revenue before any costs have been included in cost of sales.

Procedures for risk 2 (max 2 marks):

- Obtain a list of sales recorded for the new machines and compare the list to items delivered before the year-end.
- Obtain a list of inventory to ensure no items are included in revenue and inventory.
- Once this has been discussed, examine the reasons for the increase in revenue with management.
- Obtain information regarding returns after the year-end to see if some of the CryoSpin's have been returned and need to be removed from revenue.

Risk 3 (max 2 marks):

- There is a risk that receivables may be overstated in the financial statements.
- This is supported by an increase in receivables collection period from 84 days to 112 days.

- This risk may be due to sales being recognised too early on the new machines if the full sale is being recognised before despatch.

- The receivables may also be overstated due to some outstanding balances not being paid following the CryoSpin issue.

- There are also concerns over the recoverability of amounts following financial problems in the sector.

Procedures for risk 3 (max 2 marks):

- Inspect the aged receivables ledger to assess if any balances appear significantly over their payment terms.

- For any overdue balances, inspect correspondence with the customer to see if they have registered a complaint following the CryoSpin issue.

- Inspect publicly available documentation regarding outstanding balances to see if any customers have declared financial problems.

- Enquire with management to assess any ongoing discussions with outstanding customers.

- If sales of the new machine have been recognised before despatch, ensure the outstanding receivable is reversed as well as the deposit received.

- For any new customers in the year, obtain details of any credit checks performed.

- Ascertain whether any payments have been received from receivables after the year-end.

Risk 4 (max 2 marks):

- Inventory could be overstated due to the problems with the CryoSpin.

- Inventory turnover period has increased from 163 days to 222 days which could suggest that there is a high amount of CryoSpin which cannot be sold.

- As some CryoSpin machines have been sold at a discount, there is a risk that inventory has a lower NRV than the cost and needs to be written down.

- Inventory for the new machines could be classed as work-in-progress, which could be difficult to assess in terms of value due to the complex nature of the machines.

- Inventory may be understated if customers have since sent back CryoSpin machines following the criticism.

Procedures for risk 4 (max 2 marks):

- Consider employing an expert to review the status of any work-in-progress due to its technical nature.

- Examine if any CryoSpin machines have been sold post year-end below cost.

- Examine if any CryoSpin machines were returned post year-end and need to be included within inventory.

MOCK ASSESSMENT ANSWERS: SECTION 4

(d) Identify whether each of the following documents should be kept in the Permanent Audit Files (PAF) or the Current Audit Files (CAF).

Document	PAF ✓	CAF ✓
Current year bank statements		✓
Articles of incorporation	✓	
Lease agreements	✓	

(3 marks)

(e) Identify whether the following statements about recording techniques are true or false.

Statement	True ✓	False ✓
Narrative notes offer detailed explanations of internal controls.	✓	
Questionnaires allow for comprehensive details about internal controls.		✓
Flowcharts are suitable for both simple and complex processes.	✓	
Questionnaires are generally quicker to prepare and administer than narrative notes and flowcharts.	✓	

(4 marks)

AAT: AUDIT AND ASSURANCE

TASK 4 (20 MARKS)

This task is about procedures for obtaining sufficient and appropriate audit evidence.

(a) Identify which of the following the auditor will be gaining assurance on by attending the inventory count. Select true or false for each option.

Statement	True ✓	False ✓
The existence of inventory.	✓	
The effectiveness of the company's controls over the inventory count.	✓	

(2 marks)

(b) Identify the type of sampling identified below.

Description	Haphazard sampling ✓	Systematic sampling ✓	Monetary Unit sampling ✓
Selecting 30 items without specific characteristic or bias.	✓		
Selecting the balance every time the total crosses £10,000.			✓
The auditor selects every 10th balance.		✓	

(3 marks)

(c) Identify whether the statements below are true or false.

Statement	True ✓	False ✓
Original documents are a better source of evidence than copies.	✓	
Client-produced evidence is the most reliable source of evidence.		✓
Auditors only perform substantive procedures if controls are deficient.		✓

(3 marks)

MOCK ASSESSMENT ANSWERS: SECTION 4

(d) (i) Discuss THREE problems with the work carried out by your colleague. **(3 marks)**

(ii) Suggest TWO additional follow up procedures that they should perform. **(2 marks)**

Problems and suggested further procedures
Indicative content (1 mark per identified problem and 1 mark per suggested follow up procedure):
• European items have been excluded from the sample. These could present higher risk of misstatement due to potential translation issues and delivery times.
• A sample has been selected which is smaller than the firm's policy so could increase the risk of not detecting material misstatements.
• One of the items in the sample has been changed at the client's request. This is a problem as the balance could contain a fraud or error and the client could be hiding this.
• One balance is overdue (Blok Ltd). The explanation from Sylvia may be correct but your colleague needs to make further enquiries to corroborate this.
• The sale to Timb Ltd appears to have been in 20X3 so should not be recognised as a sale during the year, meaning that revenue and receivables are overstated. Your colleague should recommend that this is corrected. Even though this is not individually material, there could be other transactions like this.
• This misposting could result in other inaccurate receivables balances. This may mean the total is not misstated but could lead to problems over the collection of some items if Warm Ltd does not know the correct amounts owed from each customer.
• Overall, your colleague appears too trusting of the client responses and has not sought to obtain sufficient evidence to corroborate the explanation or confirm the outstanding balance.
• There are a number of material errors in the sample and your colleague has not proposed any further work over receivables.
Suggested follow up procedures:
• Increase the sample size selected so it is in line with the firm's policies.
• Select some European balances to test as these carry a different risk to the UK-based ones.
• Ensure R&F Ltd is included in the balance and inspect the documentation surrounding the dispute.
• Inspect correspondence from R&F Ltd as it could suggest the balance is not recoverable.
• Inspect the history of payments from Blok Ltd to assess if they have a history of paying late to corroborate Sylvie's explanation.
• Enquire as to whether Blok Ltd pay the balance prior to the completion of the audit.
• Select a sample of January despatch notes to see if there are other items like the sale to Timb Ltd which suggest an overstatement of revenue and receivables.
• Enquire as to whether there are any other instances of misallocated payments perhaps by looking for balances with a credit balance or any large overdue amounts.
• Due to the large number of issues noted, it is suggested that your colleague extends the sample as it appears that the balance is materially misstated.

(e) **Explain TWO tests of control which could be performed over the payroll process of adding employees to the payroll to ensure it is operating effectively.**

When asked to explain, students are expected to state the procedure and the audit objective of the procedure. Maximum 2 marks per procedure. **(4 marks)**

| Tests of control
Indicative content: | Audit objective i.e. why it is needed to be carried out
Indicative content: |
|---|---|
| Select a sample of individuals and inspect evidence of a valid form of ID held on file. (1) | This is to ensure that only legitimate employees are being added to the payroll, reducing the risk of 'ghost employees'. (1)
OR
To check that the company's policies and procedures for adding new employees to the payroll are being followed consistently. (1) |
| Select a sample from the joiners in the year and inspect their completed joiner form. (1) | To check that all required information has been accurately captured and recorded e.g. personal details, bank account information. (1) |
| Seek evidence of authorisation on the joiner form from the Payroll Director or other board member. (1) | This is to ensure that only approved and legitimate additions to the payroll are made to prevent unauthorised or fraudulent additions. (1)
OR
To ensure compliance with policies and procedures. Authorisation from a senior executive indicates that the process adheres to established guidelines. (1) |

(f) **Match the statement with the type of internal control it is describing.** **(3 marks)**

Internal control	Assertion
Conducting monthly reconciliations of bank statements.	A detective control
Employee A is responsible for approving purchase orders and invoices from suppliers and that the goods have been received. Employee B records the approved invoices into the accounting system. Employee C processes the payment for the recorded invoices.	A preventative control
Using software to monitor and log access to sensitive data by employees.	A detective control

MOCK ASSESSMENT ANSWERS: SECTION 4

TASK 5 (15 MARKS)

This task is about procedures for obtaining sufficient and appropriate audit evidence.

(a) Complete the following statement about evidence gathering:

Auditors must gather sufficient appropriate evidence to support their audit opinion. Sufficiency relates to the _____GAP 1_____ of evidence whereas appropriate relates to the relevance and _____GAP 2_____ of evidence.

Gap 1	✓
reliability	
reasonableness	
quantity	✓

Gap 2	✓
reasonableness	
reliability	✓
quantity	

(2 marks)

(b) Identify whether the following statements are true or false.

Statements	True ✓	False ✓
Having an internal audit function forms part of the control environment of an entity.	✓	
Auditors inspecting invoices for authorisation is a test of control.	✓	
The client preparing monthly supplier reconciliations is a test of control.		✓

(3 marks)

(c) Match the audit test to be performed over the inventory balance with the assertion they will provide evidence on.

Test	Assertion
Selecting a sample of post year-end sales to ensure items sold above cost.	Valuation
Selecting a sample of goods in the warehouse and agreeing purchase invoice stating that the goods belong to Flip Ltd.	Rights and obligations
Examining the disclosures made and ensuring that the inventory balance is categorised between raw materials, work-in-progress and finished goods.	Presentation
Selecting a sample of goods from the inventory listing and tracing them to the warehouse floor.	Existence

(4 marks)

KAPLAN PUBLISHING

AAT: AUDIT AND ASSURANCE

(d) **Identify which TWO of the following substantive audit procedures provide the most appropriate evidence of the existence of trade receivables.**

Procedure	✓
Selecting a sample of goods despatch notes signed by the customer as received.	✓
Selecting a sample of sales invoices sent to the client.	
Circularising a sample of trade receivable balances asking them to confirm the amounts owed to the client.	✓
Obtaining a breakdown of the receivables balance from the sales ledger.	

(2 marks)

(e) **Identify whether the following statements are true or false.**

Statement	True ✓	False ✓
Test data is used to test the automated controls within a client's system.	✓	
Data analytics allows auditors to test large quantities of data quickly.	✓	
A photocopy is a better source of evidence than an original document.		✓
Analytical procedures should only be used during the evidence gathering stage of the audit.		✓

(4 marks)

TASK 6 (15 MARKS)

This task is about reviewing and reporting findings and audit opinions.

(a) Explain the issues arising, any further work required and the potential impact on the audit report of Wails Ltd. **(9 marks)**

Issues arising and impact on audit report
Indicative content (1 mark per point, as shown):
There is clearly an issue that receivables are overstated by a material amount as this is unlikely to be recoverable. **(1)** This would be an adjusting event and the Wails Ltd financial statements should be altered as it appears that Sute Ltd was experiencing financial difficulty at 31 December 20X2 due to the presence of the administrators in early January. **(1)** We could examine any correspondence with the liquidators to assess if any amount is recoverable from Sute Ltd to assess how much receivables are overstated by. **(1)**
A bigger issue is perhaps that regarding Wails Ltd's ability to continue as a going concern. **(1)** Enquiries will need to be made to assess whether Wails Ltd can continue without Sute Ltd as a customer. This could involve looking at the possibility of alternative customers. **(1)** In addition to this, we will have to assess whether Wails Ltd can find alternative suitable premises, within budget. **(1)** We could inspect cash flow forecasts and compare the potential rental cost of equivalent properties to the cash flow of Wails Ltd. **(1)**
Auditor's report
If Wails Ltd fail to adjust the receivables balance, there will be a material error. **(1)** This would lead to a modified report **(1)** with a qualified opinion **(1)** due to a material misstatement. A basis for qualified opinion paragraph would be included **(1)** and the opinion would state 'except for' **(1)**, explaining the material misstatement in the receivables balance.
As Wails Ltd is no longer a going concern without the custom and property from Sute Ltd, then we will issue an adverse opinion **(1)** due to the error being material and pervasive **(1)**. This would state that the financial statements are prepared on the wrong basis as they should be prepared on a break-up basis **(1)**.

(b) Identify the appropriate action in each of the following situations.

Situation	Do nothing ✓	Speak to manager ✓
During the inventory count, you noticed a small batch of damaged goods in the warehouse. After speaking to the Financial Controller, they have not written them down as they believe that they can sell them. They are valued at £3,000 in the financial statements.	✓	
You have discovered an invoice for consulting services for £4,000. Upon investigation you have found that the consulting company is owned by the husband of the Finance Director. No disclosures have been made in the financial statements.		✓

(2 marks)

(c) **Match the following statement with the opinions from the picklist below.**

Statement	Opinion
The auditor does not express an opinion on the financial statements.	Disclaimer of opinion
The financial statements do not give a true and fair view.	Adverse opinion
Except for the matter identified in the basis for modification paragraph, the financial statements give a true and fair view.	Qualified opinion

(3 marks)

(d) **Identify whether the following statement is true or false.**

Statement	True ✓	False ✓
A modified audit report always means that the opinion is modified.		✓

(1 mark)

MOCK ASSESSMENT ANSWERS: **SECTION 4**

TASK 6 (15 MARKS)

This task is about reviewing and reporting findings and audit opinions.

(a) **Explain the issues arising, any further work required and the potential impact on the audit report of Wails Ltd.** **(10 marks)**

Issues arising and impact on audit report
Indicative content (1 mark per point, as shown)
There is clearly an issue that receivables are overstated by a material amount as this is unlikely to be recoverable. **(1)** This would be an adjusting event and the Wails Ltd financial statements should be altered as it appears that Sute Ltd was experiencing financial difficulty at 31 December 20X2 due to the presence of the administrators in early January. **(1)** We could examine any correspondence with the liquidators to assess if any amount is recoverable from Sute Ltd to assess how much receivables are overstated by. **(1)**
A bigger issue is perhaps that regarding Wails Ltd's ability to continue as a going concern. **(1)** Enquiries will need to be made to assess whether Wails Ltd can continue without Sute Ltd as a customer. This could involve looking at the possibility of alternative customers. **(1)** In addition to this, we will have to assess whether Wails Ltd can find alternative suitable premises, within budget. **(1)** We could inspect cash flow forecasts and compare the potential rental cost of equivalent properties to the cash flow of Wails Ltd. **(1)**
Auditor's report
If Wails Ltd fail to adjust the receivables balance, there will be a material error. **(1)** This would lead to a modified report **(1)** with a qualified opinion **(1)** due to a material misstatement. A basis for qualified opinion paragraph would be included **(1)** and the opinion would state 'except for' **(1)**, explaining the material misstatement in the receivables balance.
As Wails Ltd is no longer a going concern without the custom and property from Sute Ltd, then we will issue an adverse opinion **(1)** due to the error being material and pervasive **(1)**. This would state that the financial statements are prepared on the wrong basis as they should be prepared on a break-up basis. **(1)**

(b) **Identify the appropriate action in each of the following situations.**

Situation	Do nothing ✓	Speak to manager ✓
During the inventory count, you noticed a small batch of damaged goods in the warehouse. After speaking to the Financial Controller, they have not written them down as they believe that they can sell them. They are valued at £3,000 in the financial statements.	✓	
You have discovered an invoice for consulting services for £4,000. Upon investigation you have found that the consulting company is owned by the husband of the Finance Director. No disclosures have been made in the financial statements.		✓

(2 marks)

(c) Match the following statement with the opinions from the picklist below.

Statement	Opinion
The auditor does not express an opinion on the financial statements.	Disclaimer of opinion
The financial statements do not give a true and fair view.	Adverse opinion
Except for the matter identified in the basis for modification paragraph, the financial statements give a true and fair view.	Qualified opinion

(3 marks)